Date Due

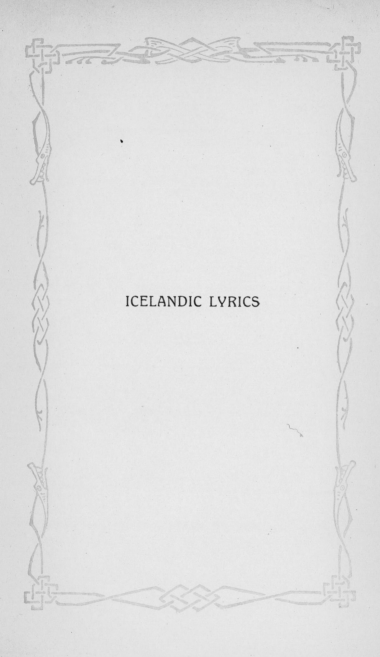

ICELANDIC LYRICS

ÍSLENZK LJÓÐ

FRUMKVÆÐI OG ÞÝÐINGAR

VALIÐ OG BÚIÐ UNDIR PRENTUN

HEFUR

RICHARD BECH

PRÓFESSOR Í NORÐURLANDAMÁLUM OG
BÓKMENNTUM VIÐ NORÐUR DAKOTA HÁSKÓLA

MEÐ MYNDUM

REYKJAVÍK MCMXXX
ÚTGEFANDI: ÞÓRHALLUR BJARNARSON
REYKJAVÍK POSTHÓLF 1001

ICELANDIC LYRICS

ORIGINALS AND TRANSLATIONS

SELECTED AND EDITED

BY *Beck*

RICHARD BECH

PROFESSOR OF SCANDINAVIAN LANGUAGES AND
LITERATURES IN THE UNIVERSITY OF NORTH DAKOTA

ILLUSTRATED

REYKJAVÍK MCMXXX
PUBLISHER: ÞÓRHALLUR BJARNARSON
REYKJAVÍK POST BOX 1001

PRINTED IN ICELAND
RÍKISPRENTSMIÐJAN GUTENBERG
REYKJAVÍK

PREFACE

This volume owes its origin to the enterprise of Mr. Þórhallur Bjarnarson, the publisher. In February last year he submitted to me a tentative plan for a collection of English translations from Icelandic poetry of the last hundred years, asking me to compile and edit it. I had long felt the need of a book of this kind; in fact, I had for some time nurtured a secret hope of filling that need. Mr. Bjarnarson's proposals therefore appealed to me; and having found that scholars like Sir William A. Craigie and Professor Halldór Hermannsson approved of the idea, I decided to undertake the task of preparing the volume. I fully realized the difficulties involved; nor is the result by any means all that I should have desired.

A translation is at best only an approximation. Moreover, the insistence on precision of form in Icelandic poetry makes the task of the translator unusually difficult. Alliteration has long been and still is a characteristic feature of Icelandic poetry; and the alliterative letters occur in the line according to strict rules. In addition, internal rhymes are frequent, to say nothing of end rhymes. Nearly all of the translators represented in this volume have refrained from attempting to reproduce the alliteration of the originals; in most cases they have, however, retained the original verseforms. It is hardly necessary to add that it is well nigh impossible to render satisfactorily into a foreign tongue the poems by the most original and the most Icelandic lyric poets.

A word about the contents of the volume. It is far from being fully representative of Icelandic poetry from the period which it covers. I had only a limited number of translations to choose from; furthermore, I included those renditions alone which I considered at least fairly successful in spirit, thought, and form. I was much more concerned with quality than quantity. Lack of space also excluded poems of any considerable length. As far as possible I did, however, select the poems most distinctly Icelandic and most characteristic of the author. I deeply lament that in several cases this could not be done owing to the lack of material at hand. Thus none of Bjarni Thorarensen's and Matthías Jochumsson's obituary pieces are included, nor any of Grímur Thomsen's or Einar Benediktsson's greatest efforts. It is also a matter of regret that some poets of merit could not be represented, as English translations of their poems were either unavailable or unacceptable. Nevertheless, the volume contains enough specimens to give the reader a fair idea of Icelandic lyric of the last hundred years as well as of the poets themselves.

In conclusion I wish to express my gratitude to all those who have aided me in my work; to the translators, or others representing them, for their co-operation; to Miss Hanna Astrup Larsen, editor of *The American-Scandinavian Review*, for allowing the reprinting of the following poems: »At Close of Day«, »Our Native Tongue«, »The Grave«, »Providence«, »Peace of God«, »Nearing Cold Dale«, »The Kiss«, and »A Sonnet«; to the *Poet-Lore* Company for permission to use the translations by Vilhjalmur Stefansson; and to Sir William A. Craigie, of the University of Chicago, Professor Skuli Johnson, of the University of Manitoba, Reverend B. B. Jónsson, D. D., of Winnipeg, Dr. Stefán Einarsson, of Johns Hopkins University, and Dr. Gudmund J. Gíslason, of Grand Forks, for suggestions and criticism. I am especially indebted to Professor Halldór Hermannsson, of Cornell University, for ready assistance and kindly encouragement throughout the preparation of the book.

The drawings are made by the artist Tryggvi Magnússon of Reykjavík.

It is the sincere hope of both the publisher and the editor that this volume may, in spite of its shortcomings, increase the interest of English-speaking people in Icelandic poetry and Icelandic literature generally.

Richard Beck.

The University of North Dakota,
Grand Forks, North Dakota,
January 15, 1930.

CONTENTS

15

INTRODUCTION

Genuine literary interest has ever characterized the Icelandic nation. This interest has not least expressed itself in love of poetry and in appreciation of the art of poetry, of perfection in metre and diction. Moreover, poetic talent, especially a ready ability of versifying, has been and still is unusually common in Iceland, among all classes of the people. Even when the national life was at its lowest ebb, Iceland had poets of merit. Space does not, however, permit a survey of Icelandic poetry down through the ages. We can only attempt a brief review of the last hundred years. During this period Icelandic literature has flourished abundantly; and it is now more varied than ever. This is particularly true of the last half century. Novelists, writers of short stories, and dramatists are numerous. Yet, the poets still hold a prominent place. Their number is legion. Only the more important will here be considered.

The nineteenth century is of special importance in the history of Icelandic literature generally, and even more so in the history of Icelandic poetry. This period was one of general national awakening, politically and intellectually. Naturally, the literature was affected by the new currents of thought which swept the country. It is even customary to speak of a renaissance in Icelandic letters during this era. At any rate, no one will deny that the national awakening produced a richer literature than Iceland had possessed for centuries. Both the renewed interest in ancient Icelandic writings and vitalizing foreign influences played here a part. Lyric poetry flourished especially.

The first poet of the nineteenth century, and one of the greatest, was Bjarni Thorarensen. He introduced romanticism into Icelandic poetry. As a student at the University of Copenhagen he had come under the influence of the Danish poet Oehlenschläger who was the leader of the romantic movement in Denmark. Nevertheless, Thorarensen owed still more to ancient Icelandic poetry, in particular the Eddic poems. He not only frequently uses the old verseforms, but he succeeds exceptionally well in reproducing the spirit of the old poems. He is more concerned with the contents than with the form of his poetry. Vigor, depth of thought, and rich imagery characterize his best poems. He wrote much accasional poetry, and his obituary pieces are both powerful and original. His patriotic poems and his love poems are also outstanding. With the name of Thorarensen is coupled that of Jónas Hallgrímsson, although the two are in many ways a contrast. Hallgrímsson excelled in exquisite lyric form; his poems are written in a simple and flowing style. His diction is unusually pure and he was a powerful force in the movement for the purification of the Icelandic language. He was a romanticist, deeply influenced by Heine, but there is much classical restraint in his poems. He, too, owed not a little to old Icelandic poetry. By profession he was a natural scientist, and he had a keen eye for the peculiar beauties of Iceland, throughout which he had travelled extensively. He wrote descriptive poems of unusual charm. Love of his native land, its beauty and its history, permeates his poetry. He is still one of his nation's most popular poets; and he has had great influence on succeeding writers.

Other important poets of the first half of the nineteenth century were Sigurður Breiðfjörð (1798 —1846) and Jón Thoroddsen. Breiðfjörð carried on with great success the tradition of the rímur-poetry. He also wrote shorter poems and epigrams. Many of the latter are veritable gems, fraught with deep feeling, tersely but excellently expressed, or containing striking pictures. He has influenced later Icelandic writers. Thóroddsen is of first importance as a novelist — the Icelandic pioneer in that field. As a lyric poet he lacks depth and originality. Nevertheless, he wrote smooth and graceful verses; and he has a refreshing sense of humor. Several of his poems are still very popular. Hjálmar Jónsson (Bólu-Hjálmar) belongs with these writers, although he outlived them by a quarter of a century. He was endowed with great poetic genius, which the most adverse of circumstances tended but to strengthen. His life-long struggle with poverty, and the lack of understanding on the part of his contemporaries, embittered him, however. His poems, therefore, often take the form of laments and scathing denunciation of his age. They are, none the less, rich in striking originality and rugged force. Jónsson can be supremely eloquent, and his darts never miss the mark.

During the latter part of the nineteenth century, a number of gifted poets carried on, more or less, the traditions of Thórarensen and Hallgrímsson.

The influence of romanticism is seen in the works of these poets, combined with strong national feeling. Not infrequently do they find inspiration and subject-matter in the sagas and the history of their country. Grímur Thomsen was at his best in historical and narrative poems. He depicts powerfully unique historical characters. His descriptions of external nature are vivid; his style is vigorous and clear-cut. Although a widely travelled man and a cosmopolitan, he is profoundly Icelandic. Benedikt Gröndal was the most thorough-going romanticist among Icelandic poets. His poems are uneven; the best ones reveal bold imagination and whimsicality. His style is lofty, at times excessively elaborate. Gísli Brynjúlfsson (1827—1888) wrote especially political poems, love songs, and occasional pieces. He was a great lover of freedom, writing beautiful poems on that subject. He was not, however, an original writer. Steingrímur Thorsteinsson won wide popularity with his graceful lyrics. He is most successful in his patriotic poems, descriptions of scenery, love songs, and satirical epigrams. Matthias Jochumsson is generally looked upon as the greatest Icelandic poet of the century. He was unusually many-sided and productive, and retained his mental powers until his dying day. He wrote on a great variety of themes. His poems on subjects from Icelandic history are particularly noteworthy, as are his elegiac and and memorial poems. At his best he combines startling imagery with profound thought; his style is eloquent and forceful. Kristján Jónsson was a poet of great promise, but died before reaching maturity. His poems are melancholy and pessimistic. At times his workmanship is faulty, but he wrote several pieces of high quality both in thought and form. Jón Ólafsson wrote glowing patriotic poems and exhortations to his countrymen. Love of his country and love of freedom are the strongest notes in his poetry. His brother, Páll Ólafsson, belongs in this group of poets, although he carries on a different tradition. Like Bólu-Hjálmar he was a peasant, and he "represents in perfection the best qualities of the unschooled Icelandic poet" (Craigie). His verses are very spontaneous, frequently humorous or satirical in character. He also wrote convivial songs and charming love poems. He is a master of the Icelandic quatrain (ferskeytla). His poems still retain their popularity.

In 1882 four Icelandic students in Copenhagen founded the periodical Verðandi. These young authors had come under the influence of George Brandes; and through their new organ made themselves the champions of realism in literature. Two of the group, Gestur Pálsson and Einar H. Kvaran, are primarily significant as novelists, although both also wrote good poetry. A third one, Hannes Hafstein, was a very gifted lyric poet. Vigor, freshness, and youthful ardor are his outstanding qualities. His descriptive poems are both vivid and powerful. His spirited exhortations, patriotic poems, and love songs are of great merit. Þorsteinn Erlingsson, though not a member of the Verðandi-group, was a self-acknowledged follower of Brandes and his realism. Erlingsson was a radical both in religion and politics; he denounced fiercely religious bigotry and social injustice. In many of his poems he expresses his views fervently and eloquently. He has the tenderest sympathy for all living things, for the weak and the suffering. He also wrote exquisite patriotic lyrics and nature poems. He was a master craftsman, and his perfection of form has won general admiration. One of his favorite verseforms was the quatrain, which he used with rare success. Through his views, and no less because of his lyric art, he has had tremendous influence.

Brief as our account of nineteenth century Icelandic poetry necessarily is, it shows at least that Iceland produced during that period an unusually large group of gifted lyric poets.

And poets continue to flourish in Iceland. Every year adds new names to the already long list. Only the most prominent of present-day Icelandic lyric poets will, however, be mentioned. Among the older ones the following deserve to be named: Þorsteinn Gíslason, Sigurjón Friðjónsson (1867), Guðmundur Friðjónsson, Guðmundur Magnússon, Guðmundur Guðmundsson, Sigurður Sigurðsson (1879), and Jóhann Sigurjónsson. The last named, renowned as a dramatist, also wrote lyric poems of a high order. Any adequate account and estimate of the works of these writers is out of the question in our limited space. Einar Benediktsson is commonly regarded as the greatest Icelandic poet now living. He has been called an Icelandic Browning, and not without reason. His poems contain profound philosophical thought expressed in lofty style.

He grapples with the deepest problems of human existence. He has also written powerful descriptive and nature poems. He is a far traveller and has spent much of his life outside of Iceland ; nevertheless, he has lost none of his Icelandic characteristics. His love for Iceland, and his faith in the future and the mission of his people are written large everywhere in his poems. He is original in style as well as in the treatment of his themes, but he is not always easy to understand. Of the younger present-day Icelandic poets the following are the most outstanding: Jakob Thorarensen (1886—), Jakob Jóhannesson Smári (1889—), Stefán frá Hvítadal, Davíð Stefánsson and Jón Magnússon (1896—). All seem destined to occupy a lasting place in the literature of their country. The women are also making a noteworthy contribution to modern Icelandic poetry. Special attention may be called to the works of Unnur Benediktsdóttir (Hulda), Theodóra Thóroddsen, and the sisters Ólína and Herdís Andrésdætur.

Present-day Icelandic poets can not readily be classified according to "schools" of poetry. Many tendencies, old and new, meet in their works. Realism plays an important part, but there is also a strong national note — a new interest in folk-poetry and folk-lore. This literature is, however, too near to us for any final estimate.

No account of Icelandic poetry of the last hundred years would be complete without a mention of the contribution made by Icelandic-Americans. In Stephan G. Stephanson they possessed a truly great poet. His productivity was amazing; and he wrote on a variety of subjects. His nature poems are rich in picturesque detail and deep thought. Nor are his many poems on themes from the sagas and other Northern lore less forceful or less poetic. His love of Iceland and things Icelandic is one of the strongest notes in his poetry, although his interests were world wide. His originality is one of his chief glories. His workmanship is on the whole admirable; and his language is rich, pure and beautiful. But he is at times obscure. Other Icelandic-American poets of merit are: Kristinn Stefánsson, Þorbjörn Bjarnarson (Þorska-bítur, 1859—), Kristján N. Julíus (1860—), Jón Runólfsson (1861—), Jóhann Magnús Bjarnason (1866—), Sigurður Júlíus Jó-hannesson, Magnús Markússon (1868—), Guttormur Jónsson Guttormsson, Þor-steinn Þ. Þorsteinsson (1879—),* and Einar P. Jónsson. These men differ, of course, in their choice and treatment of themes, in their artistry. They represent various tendencies; and they do not, by any means, all deserve the same place as poets. They have, however, in their different ways, written many good poems. And we have only enumerated the most prominent of those Icelandic-Americans who have published their poems in book-form. There are many others. Clearly, the Icelanders have not lost their appreciation of poetry or their ability to write verse when they migrated to new shores.

* In the introduction dates are given for those writers only whose lives are not sketched elsewhere in the volume.

Viewed as a whole the last hundred years have been a remarkable period in the history of Icelandic poetry. And it continues to flourish despite the increasing interest in novels, short stories, and dramas. Moreover, present-day Icelandic poetry is richer both in variety of themes and in variety of verseforms than ever before. In this respect there has been a marked gain. Stephan G. Stephanson and Einar Benediktsson, to name but the two greatest, have here set a noble example; "each of these has, in different ways, shown that the traditional form of Icelandic poetry is capable of being made the vehicle of profound and sustained thought to an extent not hitherto attempted or realized" (Craigie). And the younger Icelandic poets may well follow the leadership of these men. They should strive to open up new horizons, to enrich Icelandic literature with new themes without sacrificing the precision of form so characteristically Icelandic.

BJARNI THORARENSEN
(1786—1841)

Bjarni Vigfússon Thorarensen was born at Brautarholt in the South of Iceland. He was the son of Vigfús Þórarinsson prefect (sýslumaður) of Gullbringu- and Kjósarsýsla, and later of Rangárvallasýsla. His preparatory education Thorarensen received from private tutors, and entered the University of Copenhagen at the age of seventeen. He received his degree in law in 1807. For a number of years he was a justice of the Superior Court in Iceland; and from 1833 until his death he was Sub-Governor of the North and East Quarters. His collected poems, K v æ ð i, were first published in 1847; a second edition appeared in 1884.

ÍSLAND

Eftir Bjarna Thórarensen

Þú nafnkunna landið, sem lífið oss veittir,
landið, sem aldregi skemmdir þín börn,
hvert þinnar fjarstöðu hingað til neyttir,
hún sé þér ódugnaðs framvegis vörn.

Undarlegt sambland af frosti og funa,
fjöllum og sléttum og hraunum og sjá,
fagurt og ógurlegt ertu, þá brunar
eldur að fótum þín jöklunum frá.

Fjör kenni' oss eldurinn, frostið oss herði,
fjöll sýni torsóttum gæðum að ná,
bægi, sem kerúb með sveipanda sveiði,
silfurblár ægir oss kveifarskap frá.

Þó vellyst í skipsförmum völskunum meður
vafri að landi, ég skaða ei tel,
því út fyrir kaupstaði íslenzkt í veður
ef hún sér vogar, þá frýs hún í hel.

Ef læpuskaps ódyggðir eykjum með flæða
út yfir haf vilja læðast þér að,
með geigvænum logbröndum Heklu þær hræða
hratt skaltu aftur að snáfa af stað.

En megnirðu' ei börn þín frá vondu að vara,
og vesöld með ódyggðum þróast þeim hjá,
aftur í legið þitt forna þá fara,
föðurland, áttu og hníga í sjá.

ICELAND
Translated by Skuli Johnson

Thou land of renown that didst give us life's joy,
O land that thine offspring by ease ne'er didst harm!
Still may the aloofness that thou dost enjoy
Enring thee and ward whene'er vices alarm.

Thou wonderful medley of frost and of fire
Where fell-peaks and plains, scree and ocean-
                                        waves meet,
How fair to view art thou and wondrously dire
When flames from the glaciers flow at thy feet!

Thy flames grant us vigor, thy frosts strength afford us,
Thy fells show us arduous blessings to reach;
Thy silver-hued sea, like a seraph with sword, us
E'er sever from faintness and fortitude teach.

Though Surfeit and Ease on ships foreign together
May drift to our land that no damage I call,
For venture these out into Iceland's cold weather
Beyond the town shelters they'll freeze dead withal.

If vices of weaklings, on steeds of the tide, thee
Should seek and by stealth to thy presence draw near,
With Hecla's dread flame-swords it will then
                                        betide thee
To frighten their hosts so they slink off in fear.

If warnings thine offspring avail not to chasten,
And failings amid them should flourishing be,
To find thine old resting-place, Fatherland, hasten
And hurl thee for age 'neath the depths of the sea.

VETURINN

Eftir Bjarna Thórarensen

Hver ríður svo geyst
á gullinbrúvu
háfan of hifin
hesti snjálitum,
hnálega hristanda
hrímgan makka,
eldi hreifanda
undan stálsköflum

Glóir á gunnsnörpum
grásteind brynja,
hangir ísskjöldur
hal á öxlum;
vindur stendur svalur
af veifan skálmar,
norðljósa brúskur
bylgjar á hjálmi.

Hann er riðinn frá
heimum miðnáttar,
aflbrunni alheims
og ótta munaðar;
mun ei vor una
né vellyst þar aldri,
í Segulheimum,
á Segulfjöllum.

Elli hann ei kennir,
þó eldri sé heimi
og guði jafngamall;

WINTER

Translated by Vilhjalmur Stefansson

Who rides with such fury
A fiery charger —
Through the high heavens
A horse snow-colored?
The mighty steed
From his mane tosses
Frozen flakes
That flutter earthward.

Glowing glitters
His gray armor;
On his shoulder there hangs
A shield ice-covered;
On his head he wears
The helm of terror —
The fearful Aegis'
Frosty helmet.

He comes from the hoary
Haunts of Midnight
Where the world-force flows
From the well eternal;
Where restless seas
Roar in breakers
On shores without Spring
And Summer-less rocks.

He knows not of age
Though the oldest gods
Were his playmates ere

lifa mun hann öllum
lengur veröldum
og of lík þeirra líða.

Afl vex því öflga,
er hann það nálgast,
harðnar Fjörgyn
hans í faðmlögum;
hverfist í demant
dreyri hennar,
en grænló skikkju
gránar og hjaðnar.

— — — — —

Sagt er fyrir Vori
Vetur flýi;
hvergi þó hann flýr,
en færist ofar;
Vor skríður undir,
Vetrar er yfir
bringa breið,
um bláloft gnæfandi.

Aldrei hinn frægi þó
fjarlægist svo,
að hann heims
hjóláss sleppi
endum tveim,
eða yfirgefi
jarðar neitt,
það næst er himni.

The earth was fashioned;
The last world will die
And desolation
Veil the suns
Ere his way is ended.

The strong are strengthened
When his step approaches;
The soft Earth grows firm
In his fierce embraces,
The tears she wept
Are turned to diamonds
And her mourning garb
To a mantle of ermine.

— — — — —

'Tis not truly said
That when summer approaches
Winter flees
To the frozen Northland:
He broods in the heavens
While humble Spring
Leads Summer in
Through sunlit meadows;

'Tis in his hands
The earth turns daily,
In his powerful grasp
The poles are twirling;
And he leaves,
E'en a little moment,
Naught of earth
That's near to heaven;

Sést því á
sumri miðju
fjalls á skrauthnúfum
skartið vetrar —
því vill ei heldur
þiðna á vori
himinhrím
á höfði öldunga.

VESTANVINDURINN

Eftir Bjarna Thórarensen

Þú, sem, þegar vorar,
þínum hlýja anda
hlíðar steini studdra
storðar ísa fjalla
hrímþaki sviftir hörðu
og hjúpi grænum sveipar,
hefirðu, vestanvindur,
viðurtal okkar munað?

Hefirðu' of hafið spánska
heitan munað mér færa
kossinn kæru minnar
kinnrjóðrar, er þú hézt mér?

Sótta ég koss þinnar kæru
kinnrjóðrar, er ég hét þér,
bar ég hann blár yfir unnir
hið bjarta loft í gegnum,
Þó máttu því ei reiðast,
að þér hann fært getkat:

'Tis therefore we see
While summer lingers
The moutains still wear
The Winter's livery;
'Tis therefore we see
That Summer melts not
Heaven's hoar-frost
From the Head of Age.

THE WEST WIND

Translated by Jakobina Johnson

You, who in the spring-time
With impassioned wooing
Wrest the snowy covers
From their rocky moorings
In the frozen north-land,
— Clothing it in verdure, —
Are you, friendly west wind,
Mindful of your promise?

Have you o'er the ocean
Brought the kiss you pledged me
Warm with love and longing
From my southern sweet-heart?

I found your southern sweet-heart,
Received the kiss I promised,
Bore it o'er foaming billows
And through illumined spaces,
— Yet I must beg forgiveness,
For I have parted with it.

Því ég leit í lundi
lilju fagra í myrgin
bleiku höfði halla
til helfarar snúna,
blaðfögur mig beiddi
að bjarga fjörvi sínu;
gleymdi ég gefnu heiti
og gaf henni kossinn.

Færðist líf í liðna,
svo lyfti upp höfði
við ylsending ástar
og upp á mig brosti.
Þýð má þakka lífið
þinnar meyjar kossi.

UM FLJÓTSHLÍÐ

Eftir Bjarna Thórarensen

Á vori vænust meyja
vafin öll í skart;
á sumri fríð húsfreyja,
flest hjá þér er þarft;
á hausti blíð sem móðir mæt;
á vetrum fegurst línklætt lík,
lífs og dauð ágæt.

At day-break, in a forest,
I found a dying lily.
— Doomed, in the flush of morning
To pass away, unnoticed.
The frail, appealing beauty
Implored me to revive her.
— Then I forgot my promise:
Gave her the kiss you pine for.

Love, the subtle magic
Of your sweet-heart's token
Quickened every fibre —
And the fragile blossom
Smiled once more to heaven,
Lived, rejoiced and thanked me.

TO THE "RIVER'S SLOPE"

Translated by Skuli Johnson

The Springtide in finery fairest
Thy virginal form indues;
As Summer's glad wife, thou sharest
His store of abundant use;
The Autumn's ill blasts thou bearest
Like many a mother meet;
Well Winter's wan shroud thou wearest:
Thou, dead or alive, art sweet.

KYSSTU MIG

Eftir Bjarna Thórarensen

Kysstu mig, hin mjúka mær,
    þú ert sjúk
Kysstu mig, hin mjúka mær,
    því þú deyr.
Glaður drekk ég dauða
    úr rós
á vörum þín,
því skálin er svo skær.

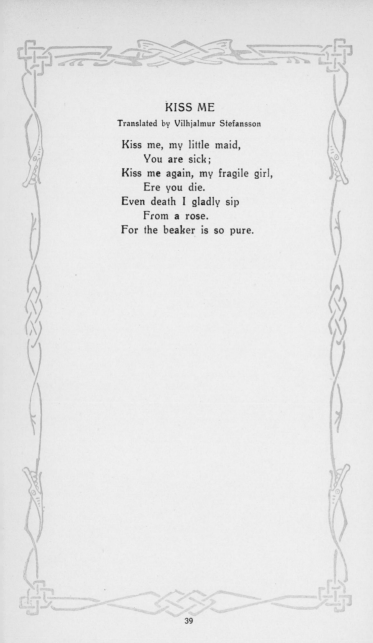

KISS ME

Translated by Vilhjalmur Stefansson

Kiss me, my little maid,
    You are sick;
Kiss me again, my fragile girl,
    Ere you die.
Even death I gladly sip
    From a rose.
For the beaker is so pure.

HJÁLMAR JÓNSSON
(1796—1875)

Hjálmar Jónsson was born at Hallandi in the North of Iceland. He never attended school, but acquired good education
through his own efforts. From 1820 until his death he was a
farmer in Skagafjörður; for a number of years, at Bóla; hence,
he is referred to as Bólu-Hjálmar. His life was a continuous
struggle with poverty and adversity. A selection from his poems,
Kvæði og kviðlingar (Poems and ditties) appeared in 1888.
A more inclusive edition was published in 1915—1919.

MANNSLÁT

Eftir Hjálmar Jónsson

Mínir vinir fara fjöld,
feigðin þessa heimtar köld;
ég kem eftir, kannske í kvöld,
með klofinn hjálm og rofinn skjöld,
brynju slitna, sundrað sverð og syndagjöld.

SAGT UPP ÚR ÞÖGN

Eftir Hjálmar Jónsson

Þekki ég óminn þessa hljóms,
þarf ei umtal meira;
nálæg þruma dauða og dóms
dunar mér við eyra.

Ber nú margt fyrir brúnaskjá,
sem betra væri að muna;
en feigum horfi ég augum á
alla náttúruna.

ELLI

Eftir Hjálmar Jónsson

Blómstrum skreyta leturs lönd
lízt mér ellin banni,
von er að stirðni helköld hönd
hálfníræðum manni.

DEATHS

Translated by Gudmund J. Gislason

Friends are taken from my sight,
Death has claimed them in the fight.
I may follow e'en tonight,
With cloven shield and helmet, bright,
Shattered mail-coat, broken sword and sin's
                                        dark blight.

SILENCE BROKEN

Translated by Gudmund J. Gislason

I know the sound o' these noises,
No need to tell how queer;
Death's and doom's thundering voices
Are booming in my ear.

Number of things I am spying,
I would recall anew;
I look with eyes a-dying
On nature's fading view.

SENILITY

Translated by Gudmund J. Gislason

With lettered bloom to grace the land,
Old age cannot contrive;
Unwieldy is the chilly hand
of man of eighty-five.

43

FEIGUR FALLANDASON

Eftir Hjálmar Jónsson

Mér er orðið stirt um stef
og stílvopn laust í höndum,
í langnættinu lítið sef,
ljós í myrkri ekkert hef,
kaldur titra krepptur gigtarböndum.

Húmar að mitt hinzta kvöld,
horfi ég fram á veginn.
Gröfin móti gapir köld,
gref ég á minn vonarskjöld
rúnir þær, sem ráðast hinumeginn.

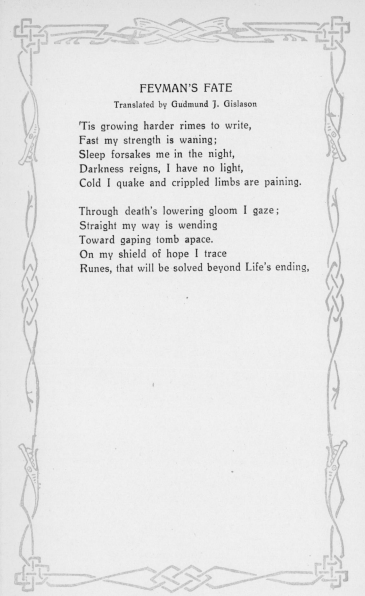

FEYMAN'S FATE

Translated by Gudmund J. Gislason

'Tis growing harder rimes to write,
Fast my strength is waning;
Sleep forsakes me in the night,
Darkness reigns, I have no light,
Cold I quake and crippled limbs are paining.

Through death's lowering gloom I gaze;
Straight my way is wending
Toward gaping tomb apace.
On my shield of hope I trace
Runes, that will be solved beyond Life's ending,

JÓNAS HALLGRÍMSSON
(1807—1845)

Jónas Hallgrímsson was born at Hraun in Öxnadal in the North of Iceland. His father was a clergyman. Hallgrímsson was graduated from the Latin School at Bessastaðir in 1829. From 1832—1837 he studied at the University of Copenhagen, principally natural science. He travelled extensively in Iceland, engaged in scientific research. He was one of the founders of the important periodical Fjölnir. (See Islandica XI, pp. 42—48). His poems, Ljóðmæli, (Poems) were published in 1847 and 1913. Some of his prose was included in Ljóðmæli og önnur rit (Poems and other writings) which appeared in 1883.

ÍSLAND

Eftir Jónas Hallgrímsson

Ísland! færsælda-frón
  og hagsælda hrímhvíta móðir!
hvar er þín fornaldar-frægð,
  frelsið og manndáðin bezt?
Allt er í heiminum hverfult,
  og stund þíns fegursta frama
lýsir sem leiftur um nótt
  langt fram á horfinni öld.

Landið var fagurt og frítt
  og fannhvítir jöklanna tindar,
himininn heiður og blár,
  hafið var skínandi bjart.
Þá komu feðurnir frægu
  og frjálsræðishetjurnar góðu
austan um hyldýpis haf
  hingað í sælunnar reit;
reistu sér byggðir og bú
  í blómguðu dalanna skauti;
ukust að íþrótt og frægð,
  undu svo glaðir við sitt.

Hátt á eldhrauni upp,
  þar sem ennþá Öxará rennur
ofan í Almannagjá,
  alþingið feðranna stóð.
Þar stóð hann Þorgeir á þingi,
  er við trúnni var tekið af lýði;
þar komu Gissur og Geir,
  Gunnar og Héðinn og Njáll.
Þá riðu hetjur um héruð,
  og skrautbúin skip fyrir landi

48

ICELAND

Translated by Guðmund J. Gislason

Iceland! gracious Frón
    and hoary magnanimous mother!
Where are thine ancient renown,
    freedom and valorous deeds?
All in the world is fleeting;
    the time of thy courtliest splendor
Flashes like lightning at night,
    afar from a bygone age.
Charming and fair was the land,
    and snow-white the peaks of the jokuls,
Cloudless and blue was the sky,
    the ocean was shimmering bright.
Then came the glorious fathers —
    the liberty's champions noble
Over the ocean's abyss
    to this blissful isle in the west;
Settled and builded their homes
    in picturesque flowery valleys,
Waxed in attainment and fame,
    contented and pleased with their lot.
High on the lava field, where
    still Oxar river is flowing
Down into Almanna gorge,
    our forefathers' Althing was held.
There in assembly stood Thorgeir
    when Christian faith was accepted.
Thither came Gissur and Geir,
    Gunnar and Hedin and Njall.
Then through the country rode heroes,
    and gorgeous ships filled the havens,

flutu með fríðasta lið,
    færandi varninginn heim.
Það er svo bágt að standa í stað,
    og mönnunum munar
annaðhvort aftur á bak
    ellegar nokkuð á leið.
Hvað er þá orðið okkar starf
    í sex hundruð sumur?
Höfum um við gengið til góðs
    götuna fram eftir veg?
Landið er fagurt og frítt,
    og fannhvítir jöklanna tindar,
himininn heiður og blár,
    hafið er skínandi bjart.
En á eldhrauni upp,
    þar sem ennþá Öxará rennur
ofan í Almannagjá,
    alþing er horfið á braut.
Nú er hún Snorrabúð stekkur,
    og lyngið á Lögbergi helga
blánar af berjum hvert ár,
    börnum og hröfnum að leik.
Ó, þér unglinga fjöld
    og Íslands fullorðnu synir!
svona er feðranna frægð
    fallin í gleymsku og dá!

GUNNARSHÓLMI
Eftir Jónas Hallgrímsson

Skein yfir landi sól á sumarvegi
og silfurbláan Eyjafjallatind
gullrauðum loga glæsti seint á degi.

Sailed by the bravest of men,
    laden with precious goods.
It is so hard to remain
    stationary without either
Slipping abackward or else
    moving a little ahead.
What has become of our labors
    of six hundred summers?
Have we been moving along
    the onward way for our weal?
Charming and fair is the land,
    and snow-white the peaks of the jokuls,
Cloudless and blue is the sky,
    the ocean is shimmering bright.
But high on the lava field, where
    still Oxar river is flowing
Down into Almanna gorge,
    Althing no longer is held.
Now Snorri's booth serves as a sheepfold,
    the ling upon Logberg the sacred
Is blue with berries each year,
    for children's and ravens' delight.
Oh, ye juvenile host
    and full-grown manhood of Iceland!
Thus is our forefathers' fame
    forgotten and dormant withal!

GUNNAR'S HOLM

Translated by Runólfur Fjeldsted

The Sun beamed o'er a land of olden story,
And Isle Mountain peak of silver-gray
Was summit-golden, — flushed with sun-set glory,

Við austur gnæfir sú hin mikla mynd
hátt yfir sveit, og höfði björtu svalar
í himinblámans fagurtærri lind.
Beljandi foss við hamrabúann hjalar
á hengiflugi undir jökulrótum,
þar sem að gullið geyma Frosti og Fjalar.
En hinumegin föstum standa fótum
blásvörtum feldi búin Tindafjöll
og grænu belti gyrð á dalamótum.
Með hjálminn skyggnda, hvítri líkan mjöll,
horfa þau yfir heiðarvötnin bláu,
sem falla niður fagran Rangárvöll;
þar sem að una byggðar býlin smáu,
dreifð yfir blómguð tún og grænar grundir.
Við norður rísa Heklu tindar háu.
Svell er á gnípu, eldur geisar undir;
í ógna djúpi, hörðum vafin dróma,
skelfing og dauði dvelja langar stundir.
En spegilskyggnd í háu lofti ljóma
hrafntinnuþökin yfir svörtum sal.
Þaðan má líta sælan sveitarblóma;
því Markarfljót í fögrum skógardal
dunar á eyrum; breiða þekur bakka
fullgróinn akur, fegurst engjaval
þaðan af breiðir hátt í hlíðarslakka
glitaða blæju, gróna blómum smám.
Klógulir ernir yfir veiði hlakka;
því fiskar vaka þar í öllum ám.
Blikar í lofti birkiþrasta sveimur,
og skógar glymja, skreyttir reynitrjám.

Þá er til ferðar fákum snúið tveimur,
úr rausnargarði hæstum undir hlíð,

East, towers that mighty shape of white array,
And cools its brow resplendent, which are laving
Cerulean-shining fountains of the day.
On a sheer precipice, a fall is raving,
To spirits of the cliff. Beneath are hiding
Frosti and Fialar golden treasures saving.
Against them Spire Mountains stand bestriding
The land; the sable cloak their limbs enclose
Is girt with green where dales begin dividing.
With helmet glittering like driven snows,
They see blue waters form melodious choirs,
At moot in meads where Crooked River flows,
Where little hearths that burn contented fires,
Dot greening fields and lawns alive with flowers.
Northward arises Hecla with her spires;
Above grim frost; below volcanic powers:
In depths unfathomed, fettered and repining,
Death and destruction dwell unnumbered hours.
Above those sable halls flash, mirror-shining,
Their raven-flinted roofs, aloft in air.
Thence smiles prosperity the land entwining;
For Markfleet in the middle valley fair,
Booms on the ear; and where its banks are bended,
Lie full-grown fields; and fertile meadows rare
Fling up their filmy tapestries extended,
Glittering, bud-bespangled, golden-spun.
The eagle wheels with yellow talons bended,
For fishes there in all the rivers run.
The birch-thrush, like a flash in air, is flying, —
And rowan-tufted woods ring in the sun.

From the rich garth high on the fell-side lying,
Are turned twain steeds unto the distant shore,

þangað sem heyrist öldufalla eimur;
því hafgang þann ei hefta veður blíð,
sem voldug reisir Rán á Eyjasandi,
þar sem hún heyir heimsins langa stríð.
Um trausta strengi liggur fyrir landi
borðfögur skeið, með bundin segl við rá;
skínandi trjóna gín mót sjávar grandi.
Þar eiga tignir tveir að flytjast á
bræður af fögrum fósturjarðarströndum
og langa stund ei litið aftur fá,
fjarlægum ala aldur sinn í löndum,
útlagar verða vinaraugum fjær;
svo hafa forlög fært þeim dóm að höndum.
Nú er á brautu borin vigur skær
frá Hlíðarenda hám, því Gunnar ríður
atgeirnum beitta búinn, honum nær
dreyrrauðum hesti hleypir gumi fríður
og bláu saxi gyrður yfir grund —
þar mátti kenna Kolskegg allur lýði.
Svo fara báðir bræður enn um stund;
skeiðfráir jóar hverfa fram að fljóti;
Kolskeggur starir út á Eyjasund,
en Gunnar horfir hliðarbrekku móti;
hræðist þá ekki frægðarhetjan góða
óvina fjöld, þó hörðum dauða hóti.
„Sá ég ei fyrr svo fagran jarðargróða,
fénaður dreifir sér um græna haga,
við bleikan akur rósin blikar rjóða.
Hér vil ég una æfi minnar daga
alla, sem guð mér sendir. Farðu vel,
bróðir og vinur!" — Svo er Gunnars saga.

*   *   *

54

Whence breakers' echoes undulate in dying:
Not e'en still days becalm the billow's roar,
On Isle Sand, where mighty ocean wages
His unremembered, elemental war.
A trusty hawser to the shore engages
A fair-built ship with sails furled to the mast;
A flashing ship's-head 'gainst all danger rages.
Thereon twain brothers are to leave, at last.
Their native shores with yearning they are viewing,
Estranged to be from them till years are past,
In alien countries days of exile ruing,
There never homefelt kindness to abide:
Such is the cruel doom the fates were brewing.
A glorious hero now away doth ride:
Gunnar from lofty Lithend is departed
Armed with his whetted halberd. By his side,
On sorrel steed, the selfsame road has started
One with a sabre blue unto him bound;
There all might Coalbeard ken, the noble-hearted.
So both the brothers journey o'er the ground:
Swift-footed coursers hurry to the river.
And Coalbeard gazes out on Isle Sound,
But Gunnar, where the fells in hazes shiver.
The famous hero, then, with spirit glowing,
Neither at foes nor death doth blanch or quiver.
"Ne'er fields grew such unearthly beauty showing;
White flocks cloud meadows green in summer glory;
'Gainst yellow fields the reddened rose is blowing.
Here will I live, e'en should my grave be gory, —
Live all days God may send. Now fare thee well
Brother and friend." So runs brave Gunnar's story,

*   *   *

Því Gunnar vildi heldur bíða hel
en horfinn vera fósturjarðar ströndum.
Grimmlegir féndur, flárri studdir vél,
fjötruðu góðan dreng í heljarböndum.
Hugljúfa samt ég sögu Gunnars tel,
þar sem ég undrast enn á köldum söndum
lágan að sigra ógna bylgju ólma
algrænu skrauti prýddan Gunnarshólma.
Þar sem að áður akrar huldu völl,
ólgandi Þverá veltur yfir sanda;
sólroðin líta enn hin öldnu fjöll
árstrauminn harða fögrum dali granda;
flúinn er dvergur, dáin hamra tröll,
dauft er í sveitum, hnipin þjóð í vanda;
en lágum hlífir hulinn verndar kraftur
hólmanum, þar sem Gunnar sneri aftur.

ÉG BIÐ AÐ HEILSA

Eftir Jónas Hallgrímsson

Nú andar suðrið sæla vindum þýðum;
á sjónum allar bárur smáar rísa
og flykkjast heim að fögru landi Ísa,
að fósturjarðar minnar strönd og hlíðum.

Ó! heilsið öllum heima rómi blíðum
um hæð og sund í drottins ást og friði;
kyssi þið, bárur! bát á fiskimiði,
blási þið, vindar! hlýtt á kinnum fríðum.

Not e'en grim death could Gunnar's heart compel
To leave his homeland fair for lands asunder,
But ruthless foes, with treachery most fell,
Slew a man good and true in battle-thunder.
And yet his heartfelt story is a spell,
Where on the chilling sands I pace and wonder,
That in the wild surge furiously driving,
Still, Gunnar's Holm is verdantly surviving.
Where there of yore a fertile field was spread,
Cross River rolls in angry perturbation.
Sun-flushed, the olden mountains see, with dread,
The valley meadows suffer mutilation.
The dwarf is flown; the fairy-folk are dead;
Gloom in the land, and droops the weary nation;
A hidden hand still keeps in verdant glory,
The holm, where Gunnar turned in olden story.

A GREETING

Translated by Jakobina Johnson

The balmy south a gentle sigh releases —
And countless ocean billows, set in motion,
Breathe to my native shores the south's devotion, —
Where strand and hillside feel the kindly breezes.

O give them all at home my fondest greeting,
O'er hill and dale a sacred peace and blessing.
Ye billows, pass the fisher's boat caressing;
And warm each youthful cheek, ye south winds
fleeting.

Vorboðinn ljúfi, fuglinn trúr, sem fer
með fjaðrabliki háa vegaleysu
í sumardal að kveða kvæðin þín;

heilsaðu einkum, ef að fyrir ber
engil með húfu' og rauðan skúf, í peysu;
þröstur minn góður! það er stúlkan mín.

Herald of springtime, thou whose instinct free,
Pilots thy shiny wings through trackless spaces
To summer haunts to chant thy poems rare.

O greet most fondly, if you chance to see
An angel whom our native costume graces.
For that, dear throstle, is my sweetheart fair.

JÓN THORODDSEN
(1819—1868)

Jón Þórðarson Thoroddsen was born at Reykhólar in the
West of Iceland. His father was a cooper. Thoroddsen graduated from the Latin School at Bessastaðir in 1840. He then
spent many years in Copenhagen, interesting himself in diverse
activities besides his law study. For a while he even served
as a volunteer in the Danish army. He completed his law
studies in 1854. He was prefect of Barðastrandarsýsla and later
of Borgarfjarðarsýsla until his death. His poems, Kvæði,
were published in 1871; an enlarged edition appeared in 1919.
Thoroddsen was Iceland's pioneer novelist.

Á SVÍNADAL

Eftir Jón Thoroddsen

Ó, fjalladalur, fögrum vaxinn smárum,
og fífilskrauti báðar settar hlíðir!
þið hermið mér um horfnar fyrri tíðir,
er hjarta mitt var engum lostið sárum.

Hér sleit ég fyrstu æfi minnar árum
og unni lífi, varð þá fátt að meini,
utan er grét ég gráum undir steini
hinn góða Kjartan sönnum vinar tárum.

Eins eruð þér sem áður, hnjúkar fríðu!
en eg er breyttur, skýjum myrkvuð gleði,
af augum hrynja ekki dropar tára;
þeir voru synir sakleysis og blíðu —
ég sakna þeirra — léttu ungu geði —
en króknuðu við kuldanepju ára.

UNDIR SVÖRTULOFTUM

Eftir Jón Thoroddsen

Hér dimmur vakir dauði langar nætur
og daga alla, björgum undir svörtum,
í hendi ógnarbrandi veifar björtum,
og boðað skelfing veiku fjöri lætur.
En alda voleg ólmast hans við fætur
og afli þungu kletta lemur harða
og liðnum yfir líkum reisir varða
úr löðri hvítu hamra upp við rætur.

Hér sefur þú í sævargrænu leiði,
þú sonur Ísajarðar hugum kæri,

ON SWINES' DALE

Translated by Skuli Jóhnson

O mountain-dale in fairest clovers clad,
And ye twin slopes adorned in daffodils!
Ye tell me of the times ere aches and ills
Enveloped me and ere a wound I had.

Here erst I lived, a little country lad,
Enjoying life and over naught made moan
Save when I, seated 'neath the old gray stone,
Shed tears for Kjartan and his ending sad.

Ye, moutains, still show forth fair eminence,
But I am changed; dark sorrows o'er me lower,—
Yet I alway withhold the welling tears.
Ye were the offspring of mild innocence —
I yearn for you that cheered my childhood hour —
But were congealed by cold and cheerless years.

'NEATH "DARKSOME FELLS"

Translated by Skuli Johnson

Here sombre Death 'neath darksome mountains dwells
Lord of brief day and lengthy northern night;
Here standeth he with blazing brand bedight
And dreads and fears to our faint hearts foretells.
Close by his feet, the awful ocean swells;
Its waves against the mountain fastness fall,
And o'er the dead erect momorial
Of white sea-foam that frets the gloomy fells.

Here sleepest thou within thine ocean-bed,
Beloved scion of our island-race,

sem banasigð í blóma lífsins felldi.
Sofðu hér rótt! og sól frá bláu heiði
saknaðarrósir þinn á legstað færi,
er sígur hún að svölum mar að kveldi!

VENUS RENNIR HÝRUM HVÖRMUM

Eftir Jón Thoroddsen

Venus rennir hýrum hvörmum
  himni bláum frá,
jörðu svefns í svölum örmum
  sjónir festir á,
inn um lítinn gægist glugga —
grímu allt er hulið skugga —
hverju ertu að að gæta
  ástargyðjan mæta?

„Þessa hetju brand í blóði
  baða' í gær ég sá,
varðist djarft hinn vígamóði,
  viður liðsmun á,
yfir mannhring öflgan stekkur,
undan fjandasveitin hrekkur.
böndum kemur á hann engi,
  að þó sæki mengi."

„Þann, sem bundið engi ýta
  áður fékk, né sært,
hefir meyjan handarhvíta
  í harðar viðjar fært;
Orkar hann ei af sér kasta
armalaga bandi fasta,
honum sem að hálsi réði
  hnýta mær á beði."

To reap whose bloom Death's ruthless sickle shone.
O rest in peace! And may the Sun's rays shed
Roses of morning on thy resting-place
When to the sea he sinks and day is done!

VENUS WITH BLITHE EYES IS BEAMING
Translated by Skuli Johnson

Venus with blithe eyes is beaming
    From the heavens blue;
Earth, in Sleep's cool arms adreaming,
    'Neath her lies to view.
"Through a little luffer peeping,
Where Night hath all in her keeping,
What, pray, art thou scrutinizing,
    Goddess love-devising?"

"Yon lad saw I yester-even
    Bathe in blood his brand,
Facing in a fight uneven
    Foes on every hand.
Over bands beleaguering leapt he
From him hosts embattled swept he,
Him enfetter could not any
    In their onslaughts many.

Him who foemen countless foiled,
    'Scaping every harm,
Hath a fair-armed lass embroiled
    In love's fett'ring charm;
He ne'er frees him from her power
Whom, within her maiden-bower,
Hath with arms so closely pressing,
    Clasped this lass caressing."

GRÍMUR THOMSEN
(1820—1896)

Grímur Þorgrímsson Thomsen was born at Bessastaðir in the South of Iceland. His father was a well-to-do farmer. Thomsen received his preparatory education from Bishop Árni Helgason. For several years he studied law, philology, aesthetics, and philosophy at the University of Copenhagen. He was granted a Master's degree, and later a Doctor's degree, for a work on Byron. During a long period Thomsen was in the Danish diplomatic service. Upon resigning his office in 1866, he went to Iceland where he was principally engaged in farming the rest of his days; but he also took an active part in politics and was a member of the Icelandic Parliament from 1869 to 1891. He was an essayist and a journalist, as well as a poet. His poems, Ljóðmæli, have been published three times, — in 1880, in 1895, and in 1906

SVERRIR KONUNGUR

Eftir Grím Thomsen

Þótt páfi mér og biskup banni,
banasæng skal konungmanni
hásætið til hvílu reitt;
kórónaður kóngur er ég,
kórónu til grafar ber ég,
hvort þeim er það ljúft eða leitt.

— — — — —

Margar fór ég ferðir glæfra,
fætur mína vafði' í næfra,
kulda mér þá sviðinn sveið.
En — hvað var það hjá hugarangri,
hverja stund á vegferð langri,
sem ég fyrir land mitt leið?

Konunglegan klætt í skrúða
kistuleggið holdið lúða,
ber sé látin ásýnd ein.
Breidd sé sigurflugu sængin,
svo til hinzta flugs ei vænginn
skorti gamlan Birkibein.

Vel er, að þér sálma syngið
og saman öllum klukkum hringið,
meðan ég skaflinn moldar klýf.
En í tilbót eitt mér veitið:
Andvökuna mikinn þeytið,
andvaka var allt mitt líf.

KING SVERRIR

Translated by Eiríkur Magnússon

The Pope and Prelate notwithstanding
Listen to a king commanding :
Let my death-bed be the throne.
Crown'd I am, and none shall stay me,
Crown'd, till in the tomb ye lay me,
'Spite them all I reign here alone.

— — — — —

Many were the hours of danger,
When I, famish'd and a stranger
Trod a cold and distant shore ;
But what were these to hours of anguish,
Banish'd for my home to languish,
All for fatherland I bore.

In my robes of state array me
When in death to rest ye lay me,
Bare my face alone shall be,
Vict'ry banner o'er me lying,
Serve the King as wings for flying
Onward to eternity.

Psalms it well behoves you singing
And also set the bells a-ringing,
While in the mould ye make my bed.
One more boon I beg, however,
Blow the 'Wakeful' loud as ever
Wakeful was the life I led.

LANDS-LAG

Eftir Grím Thomsen

Heyrið vella' á heiðum hveri,
Heyrið álftir syngja' í veri:
    Íslands er það lag.
Heyrið fljót á flúðum duna,
foss í klettaskorum bruna
    Íslands er það lag.

Eða fugl í eyjum kvaka!
undir klöpp og skútar taka:
    Íslands er það lag.
Heyrið brim á björgum svarra,
bylja þjóta svipi snarra:
    Íslands er það lag.

Og í sjálfs þín brjósti bundnar
blunda raddir náttúrunnar:
    Íslands eigið lag.
Innst í þínum eigin barmi
eins í gleði' og eins í harmi
    ymur Íslands lag.

ENDURMINNINGIN

Eftir Grím Thomsen

Endurminningin merlar æ
í mána silfri hvað, sem var,
yfir hið liðna bregður blæ
blikandi fjarlægðar,
gleðina jafnar, sefar sorg;
    svipþyrping
    sækir þing
í sinnis hljóðri borg.

ICELAND'S SONG

Translated by Jakobina Johnson

Hear the geysirs in the highlands,
Hear the swans among the islands:
    That is Iceland's song.
Streams through rocky channels sweeping
Falls through narrow gorges leaping:
    That is Iceland's song.

Song-birds 'round the shores abounding,
Lofty cliff and cave resounding:
    That is Iceland's song.
Roaring breakers shoreward crashing,
Rushing winds like spirits flashing:
    That is Iceland's song.

Deep within my bosom's keeping
Rest these sounds of nature sleeping,
    That is Iceland's own.
Breathes through every great emotion
Joy, or sorrow's troubled ocean
    Iceland's softest tone.

REMEMBRANCE

Translated by Skuli Johnson

The memory in moon-sheen shrouds
The matters of the Past;
All things that were her charm enclouds,
O'er gleaming Distance cast;
She chastens Joys, soothes Sorrows all:
    Her Shade-hosts wend
    And mote attend
In Mind's still Capitol.

Lágt þó þeir hafi, heyri' ég allt,
sem hvísla þeir í eyra mér;
segja þeir: „Verða svipur skalt
þú sjálfur, líkt og vér;
kvöldroði lífsins kenni þér,
    að kemur skjótt
    en svala nótt,
og svefn í skauti ber." —

Í æsku fram á lífsins leið
vér lítum, en ei annað neitt,
vonandi' að breiða gatan greið
grænum sé blómum skreytt;
en — aftur horfir ellin grá.
    Sólarlag
    liðinn dag
laugar í gulli þá.

SÓLHEIMASANDUR

Eftir Grím Thomsen

Svo ríddu þá með mér á Sólheimasand,
sjávar þar aldrei þagnar kliður,
en Jökulsá spinnur úr jakatoga band
og jökullinn í hafið gægist niður.

Hann horfir á starf hinnar hraðstreymu ár
og hettuna missir af skalla,
en Jökulsá hana sinn lyppar í lár
og loðið tætir reifi hvítra mjalla.

En þó er sú strönd heldur þegjandaleg,
þar heyrast ei kvikar raddir neinar,
því náttúran talar þar ein við sjálfa sig,
en sveina fæstir skilja, hvað hún meinar.

Though low they speak yet hear I all
They whisper to my ear;
They say: "Soon change to shade you shall
And e'en like us appear.
Life's ev'ning glow to you attest:
    'Soon comes to sight
    The chilly night —
She bears Sleep at her breast'."

In youth we view the way untrod
That is so dimly shown;
We hope our path all smooth and broad
With blossoms may be strown.
But back looks age, so old and sere:
    The setting sun
    Sheds gold upon
The days long passed and dear.

"SUNNY HAUNTS' SAND"
Translated by Skuli Johnson

So ride thou then with me to Sunny Haunts' Sands
Where silent is never the sea's wild commotion,
Where Glace-River weaves from the ice-floes long bands,
And Glacier-Fell downward peers to the ocean.

He sees what is wrought by the swift-coursing stream,
The cowl from his bald pate down slips as he ponders;
And Glace-Stream enrings it with eddies agleam
And cards all its snow-fleece as seawards she wanders.

Yet desolate somewhat and sad is that strand,
For voices human ne'er come there intruding,
And Nature communes there in solitude, and
To few is it given to fathom her brooding.

BENEDIKT GRÖNDAL
(1826—1907)

Benedikt Sveinbjarnarson Gröndal was born at Bessastaðir.
He was the son of Sveinbjörn Egilsson, a noted scholar and
poet. Gröndal was graduated from the Latin School at his birth-
place in 1846. He studied natural science and literature at the
University of Copenhagen, where he received a Master's degree in Norse philology in 1863. From 1874 to 1883 he was a
teacher in the College of Iceland at Reykjavík; but throughout
his life, writing was his main interest. He produced much
miscellaneous prose as well as verse. His collected poems,
Kvæðabók, appeared in 1900.

HRET

Eftir Benedikt Gröndal

Fölnuð er liljan og fölnuð er rós,
fölnað er himinsins blessaða ljós;
hnípinn er skógur og hnigið er bar,
hám sem að áður á björkunum var.

Stynja nú biturri stofnar í hríð,
stirðnaður lækur í blómlausri hlíð;
himininn fær ei að fella nein tár,
frosti hann grætur, það hagl er og snjár.

Eins ertu þornuð af augunum mín,
ástsæla táranna lind, sem að skín
annars í heiminum huggunarrík,
Himnanna drykk ertu sannlega lík!

Viðkvæma, barnslega vætti hún kinn,
var það hinn einasti huggarinn minn;
út streymdi sorgin, og inn streymdi ró,
eymdin og reiðin í hjartanu dó.

Allt eins og dögg vætir ilmblómin ung,
ofan þau hneigjast að jörðunni þung,
rísa svo aftur við eyglóar yl,
upprisin lyfta sér himinsins til:

Döggin svo harmanna brauzt mér um brár,
blikandi æskunnar huggunartár;
þá var ég ungur, ég gekk mig og grét,
gráturinn sorgina hverfa mér lét.

Lífsins á heiði í helkuldablæ
huggun ég enga af tárunum fæ;
Döggin er huggandi, þó hún sé þung,
þíðir upp líf, meðan rósin er ung.

REGRET

Translated by Jakobina Johnson

Roses and lilies have wilted away,
Summer skies changed to a shadowy gray.
Dreary the forest and leafless the trees,
Proudly that swayed in the wandering breeze.

Naked and moaning the trees meet the gale,
Still lies the brook in a desolate vale.
Gone from the heavens the warm tears that flow,
— Changed by the frost into hail-stones or snow.

Gone art thou likewise, and dry with my years,
Lovéd and comforting fountain of tears.
Blessing and soothing, — a world-healing force,
Thou wert a boon from a heavenly source.
— — — — —

Soft as the dew was thy touch on my cheek,
Solace and friend that our childhood may seek.
Peace would re-enter and sorrow depart,
Anger and pain would die out in my heart.

Soft rests the dew on the flowers at morn,
Down to the earth by its weight they are borne.
Looking again when the sun travels high,
Pure and refreshed to the beautiful sky.

Thus when the sorrows brought night to my heart,
Tears, like the dew-fall, would heavily start.
Few were my years, and that dew-fall in truth,
Driven away by the sun of my youth.
— — — — —

Out on the moors in a wintery gale,
Tears falling warm prove of little avail.
— Only our youth knows that sudden relief,
Flowery season — in passing too brief.

77

Gerðu mig aftur sem áður ég var,
alvaldi guð, meðan æskan mig bar!
Gefðu mér aftur hin gulllegu tár!
Gefðu að þau verði ekki hagl eða snjár!

NÓTT
Eftir Benedikt Gröndal

Sólin er sígin til viðar
í svalan norður straum,
blikandi bláöldur líða.
brosa við næturheimsdraum.

Máninn frá loftinu lítur
á lagar og hauðurs ró —
fram starir drangurinn dimmi
á dökkvan og skyggðan sjó.

Kyrrt er á kerlingarskerjum,
kúrir und skútanum már,
sefur á Sviðholtshólma
selurinn strykinn og grár.

Einmana í fjörunni fetar
frammi við dökkleitan sæ
mærin, sem undi sér áður
á enginu í vordagablæ.

Þar hvarf mærin hin mæra —
myrkt er í klettanna þró —
gekk hún bak við drangann hinn dimma —
eða datt hún í kolbláan sjó?

Skýldu þér ekki í skýjum,
skiftu þér ei, máni, af því
hvort stúlkan er lífs eða liðin,
læðstu geiminum í.

Heavenly Father, my childhood restore,
Make me contented and carefree once more.
Grant me those tears with their comforting flow,
— Grant that they change not to hail-stones or snow.

NIGHT

Translated by Skuli Johnson

Day's hosts have passed down yonder
'Neath West's chill ocean-streams,
And the glitt'ring blue waves wander
As quietly as dreams.

The moon on high, soft-faring,
Beholds the sleep-held lea,
And a headland grim stands staring,
Anigh the silent sea.

On Carline's Skerries tarry
Sea-mews whom caves conceal,
By the holm of Singed Hill scarry
Slumbers a gray-streaked seal.

Where Ocean's realm deploys
Beside the shore-reefs dun,
Lo, a lassie gropes: her joys
Of love's dear Spring are done.

O whither coursed that maiden?
I ask you, ghyll-clefts all.
Did she pass you, height dusk-laden,
Or mid you, blue waves, fall?

Hide not in clouds enringing,
O moon, nor have a care:
Be she dead or not, light-winging
Through heaven blithely fare.

79

PÁLL ÓLAFSSON

(1827—1905)

Páll Ólafsson was born at Dvergasteinn in the East of
Iceland. He was the son of Ólafur Indriðason, a clergyman
and poet of some ability. Ólafsson received only such education as was given in the home; he attended no school. The
greater part of his life he was a farmer. His poems, Ljóðmæli, edited by his brother, Jón Ólafsson (see later), appeared in two volumes in 1899—1900.

SUMARKVEÐJA

Eftir Pál Ólafsson

Ó, blessuð vertu, sumar-sól,
er sveipar gulli dal og hól
og gyllir fjöllin himin-há
og heiðarvötnin blá.
Nú fossar, lækir, unnir, ár
sér una við þitt gyllta hár;
nú fellur heitur haddur þinn
um hvíta jökulkinn.

Þú klæðir allt í gull og glans,
þú glæðir allar vonir manns;
og hvar sem tárin kvika' á kinn,
þau kyssir geislinn þinn.
Þú fyllir dalinn fuglasöng,
nú finnast ekki dægrin löng,
og heim í sveitir sendirðu' æ
úr suðri hlýjan blæ.

Þú frjóvgar, gleður, fæðir allt
um fjöll og dali' og klæðir allt,
og gangirðu' undir, gerist kalt,
þá grætur þig líka' allt.
Ó, blessuð vertu sumar-sól,
er sveipar gulli dal og hól
og gyllir fjöllin himin-há
og heiðarvötnin blá!

A SUMMER GREETING

Translated by Skuli Johnson

You, summer sun, we bless and hail,
You shed your gold o'er hill and dale
And gild the heaven-meeting mounts
And heath-lakes' azure founts!
Rills, springs and streams, all waves that fare,
Delight them with your golden hair,
And 'bout each glacier's hoary head
Your glowing locks you spread.

Your gold and sheen all things endue,
You kindle all men's hopes anew,
And where o'er cheeks the tears down stream
You kiss them with your gleam.
You fill the dales with birds' sweet song
So days no more are dull or long,
And to our haunts without surcease
You send the South's warm breeze.

You nurture, rear, and gladden all
'Bout fells and dales, and clothe withal;
Pass you from sight times chill ensue
And all things mourn for you.
You, summer sun, we bless and hail,
You shed your gold o'er hill and dale,
And gild the heaven-meeting mounts
And heath-lakes' azure founts!

STEINGRÍMUR THORSTEINSSON
(1831—1913)

Steingrímur Bjarnason Thorsteinsson was born at Arnarstapi in the West of Iceland. He was the son of Bjarni Thorsteinsson, Sub-Governor of the Western Quarter. Thorsteinsson was graduated from the College of Iceland in 1851. He studied philology at the University of Copenhagen and received the degree of candidatus philologiae in 1863. From 1872 until his death he was a teacher in the College of Iceland; from 1904, the rector of the College. He was extremely productive as a writer, both in prose and poetry. And he greatly enriched Icelandic literature by numerous and significant translations, including the Arabian Nights and Shakespeare's King Lear. Thorsteinsson's poems, Ljóðmæli, were first published in 1881; a second enlarged edition appeared in 1893, a third enlarged edition in 1910, and a fourth in 1925.

ÍSLAND

Eftir Steingrím Thorsteinsson

Eykonan hvít við dimblátt djúp,
er kappa vakir hrygg við hauga;
þungbúnu hrýtur hagl af auga
niður í fagran fannahjúp;
þú grætur þá, sem látnir lifa
þar ljósin Valaskjálfar bifa;
syrgjandi ber þú höfuð hátt
heiðskíra viður norðurátt.

Gengin er tíð, þá loft og lög
valkyrjur riðu í leiftra ljóma,
við sverða skin og skjaldarhljóma
og kysstu harðan hildar mög;
þegar að fleyin sköruð skjöldum,
skriðu að þínum ströndum köldum,
þá konungborið kappalið
kaus sér að deyja brjóst þitt við.

— — — — —

Kenn oss að feta í feðra spor
á ferli nýjum; móðir aldna,
að lifni storðin fönnum faldna
og nöprum fylgi vetri vor;
frá harmi snúin horfins blóma,
heið þig í nýja tímans ljóma,
og undir hjálmi ægis blá
óskmögum sýndu hýra brá.

ICELAND

Translated by William A. Craigie.

White island-dame by dark blue deeps,
That watchest sad by warrior's tomb,
From out thine eyes in upper gloom
The hail beats down on snow-bound steeps.
Thou weepest those who live though dead
Where light through heaven's halls is shed,
And sorrowing lookest proudly forth
Toward the clear skies of the North.

Gone is the time when near and far
Valkyries rode in lightning's flash,
Mid din of swords and bucklers' crash,
And kissed the hardy sons of war.
When ships with shields above their oars
Came sailing to thy frosty shores,
And heroes sprung from royal line
Chose here to die as sons of thine.

— — — — —

Teach us our fathers' steps to tread
In new achievements, mother old,
That life may come to deserts cold,
And spring succeed to winter dead.
Gaze not behind towards the past,
But forward where thy fame shall last,
And while thy helmet frowns above
Regard thy sons with eyes of love.

SVANASÖNGUR Á HEIÐI

Eftir Steingrím Thorsteinsson

Ég reið um sumaraftan einn
á eyðilegri heiði;
þá styttist leiðin löng og ströng,
því ljúfan heyrði' ég svanasöng,
já, svanasöng á heiði.

Á fjöllum roði fagur skein,
og fjær og nær úr geimi
að eyrum bar sem englahljóm,
í einverunnar helgidóm,
þann svanasöng á heiði.

Svo undurblítt ég aldrei hef
af ómi töfrazt neinum;
í vökudraum ég veg minn reið
og vissi' ei hvernig tíminn leið
við svanasöng á heiði.

SÖNGLISTIN

Eftir Steingrím Thorsteinsson

Svífðu nú sæta,
söngsins englamál!
angrið að bæta
yfir mína sál;
tónaregn þitt táramjúkt
titri nið'r á hjartað sjúkt,
eins og dala
daggir svala
þyrstri rós í þurk.

SWANSONG ON THE MOORLANDS

Translated by Jakobina Johnson

Alone, upon a summer's eve,
I rode the dreary moorlands.
— No more the way seemed bleak and long
For sudden strains of lovely song
Were borne across the Moorlands.

The mountains glowed with rosy light. —
— From far across the moorlands
And like a sacred interlude
It fell upon my solitude,
That song upon the moorlands.

It thrilled my soul with sweet response,
That song upon the moorlands.
As in a dream I rode ahead —
And knew not how the moments fled,
With swans upon the moorlands.

VOICE OF SONG

Translated by Jakobina Johnson

Come, soft and soothing —
Angel voice of song.
Anguish and sorrow
I have suffered long.
Soft as tears or falling rain,
Lightly touch my heart in pain.
　　As to flowers
　　Evening showers
Dying hopes restore.

Inndæl sem kliður
ástafugls við lind,
rammefld sem niður
reginhafs í vind
óma, sönglist, unaðsrík.
Önd mín hrifin svani lík
blítt í draumi
berst með straumi
út á hljóms þíns haf.

VIÐ HAFIÐ

Eftir Steingrím Thorsteinsson

Við hafið ég sat fram á sævar-bergs stall
    og sá út í drungann,
þar brimaldan stríða við ströndina svall
    og stundi svo þungan.

Og dimmur var ægir og dökk undir él
    var dynhamra-borgin,
og þá datt á náttmyrkrið þögult sem hel
    og þungt eins og sorgin.

„Þú haf! sem ber tímans og harmanna farg,
    þú hugraun mér vekur,
í hjarta mér innst, þá þú brýzt um við bjarg,
    það bergmála tekur.

Þinn niður er hryggur, þinn hljómur er sár,
    þú hrellir svo muna,
sem brimdropi hver væri beiskasta tár,
    hvert báruhljóð stuna.

Sweet as by fountains
Wooing birds may sing,
Deep as the echoes
Ocean winds may bring,
Let thy measures ebb and flow —
And my soul enraptured go
    Swanlike sailing,
    — Dreams prevailing —
On thy waves of sound.

BY THE SEA

Translated by Runólfur Fjeldsted

I sat on a cliff where the seas ever rave
    And gazed through the gloaming.
And heavily sighing the billowing wave
    Was falling and foaming.

The gloom of the mists and the moan of their breath
    The sea cliff did borrow;
And then fell the darkness as silent as death
    And heavy as sorrow.

"O sea, where the sad waves unquietly start,
    And dark storms assemble,
Thou strikest the innermost rocks of my heart,
    that echoing tremble.

Thy voice is so grievous and piercing to hear,
    My spirit doth sicken,
As were every brine drop the bitterest tear
    Of seas sorrow stricken.

Af aðsigi tára fá augu mín kvöl
    með ekkanum stranga.
Hér vildi ég gráta sem barn allt mitt böl
    við brimniðinn langa."

En dimmraddað hafið þá knúðist að klett,
    það klökk ei né stundi;
í hríðfelldum boðum, sem þeystust að þétt,
    það þrumaði og drundi:

„Þú, maður hinn veiki, það magn, sem ég hlaut,
    ei mæðist af kvíða;
hvað stoðar að tárast? Í þungri ber þraut
    að þola og stríða.

LAUSAVÍSUR

Eftir Steingrím Thorsteinsson

ÞREK OG VIÐKVÆMNI

Hjarta mitt stælist við stríð,
    þó stenzt á hvað vinnst og hvað tapast;
það, sem mitt þrek hefir grætt,
    það hefir viðkvæmnin misst.

VIRÐING OG ÁST

Virðing þú segist mér veita,
    svo veittu mér ást þína líka,
ilmlaust ei bjóð þú mér blóm,
    bragðfrítt þó sé það að lit.

My eyes burn with tears and my grief cannot stay
    Its panting emotion;
I would like a child weep my sorrows away,
    Where wails the sad ocean."

Then high on the cliff dashed the hollow-voiced sea,
    Not sobbing or sighing;
With swift whirling waves dashing on wild and free,
    It thundered forth, crying:

"I have, O frail mortal, a power to stay
    Unmarred by disaster;
What profit thy tears? learn, when woes come thy way,
    To bear them and master."

EPIGRAMS

Translated by Vilhjalmur Stefansson

LOSS AND GAIN

My heart is strengthened by strife,
    yet are matched my winnings and losses,
For that which in power I gain,
    that I in tenderness lose.

ESTEEM AND LOVE

I have your regard, as you say,
    but if your love be not given
'Tis a flower whose fragrance is fled,
    fair though the color may be.

GÓÐVERK

Ef góðverk þú vinnur, þá ger það af dyggð,
hreint „gratis", og heimtaðu' ei þökk eða tryggð;
einn gullhringur sé það í græðisdjúp þeyttur
ei glófagur öngull af sjálfselsku beittur.

LJÓNIÐ OG SVÍNIÐ

Svöng eru ljónin, svínin mett,
samt skal þar á minna,
að ofar ljóna auðn er sett
en alistía hinna.

GENEROSITY

If you would do good, then do it to-day,
Do it gratis, nor linger around for your pay;
Let the deed be a gem that you cast overboard,
Not a hook that is baited to fish for reward.

LIONS AND SWINE

The lion oft hungers, and yet,
Though the swine are well fed, and all that,
Higher the desert is set
Than the sty where the others grow fat.

MATTHÍAS JOCHUMSSON
(1835—1920)

Matthías Jochumsson was born at Skógar in the West of
Iceland. He was the son of an impoverished farmer. Jochumsson attended school comparatively late in life, and was graduated from the College of Iceland in 1863 and from the Theological School in 1865. From 1866 until 1900 he served as clergyman in various parts of Iceland. From 1900 and until his
death he received from the Icelandic government an honorary
pension in recognition af his literary work. He was at once
a versatile and prolific writer. He was a journalist, a noted
dramatist, as well as the leading lyric poet of his day. He, too,
enriched Icelandic literature by numerous and excellent translations, notable among which are four of Shakespeare's greatest tragedies and Byron's Manfred. Jochumsson's poems,
Ljóðmæli, first appeared in one volume in 1884, and again in
five volumes 1902—1906. A volume of selections appeared in 1915.

FORSJÓNIN

Eftir Matthías Jochumsson

Hvað er það ljós, sem lýsir fyrir mér
þá leið, hvar sjón mín enga birtu sér?
Hvað er það ljós, sem ljósið gerir bjart
og lífgar þessu tákni rúmið svart?
Hvað málar „ást" á æsku-brosin smá,
og „eilift líf" á feiga skörungs-brá?
Hvað er þitt ljós, þú varma hjartans von,
sem vefur faðmi sérhvern tímans son?
      Guð er það ljós.

Hver er sú rödd, sem býr í brjósti mér,
og bergmálar frá öllum lífsins her —
sú föður-rödd, sem metur öll vor mál,
sú móður-rödd, er vermir líf og sál —
sú rödd, sem ein er eilíflega stillt,
þótt allar heimsins raddir syngi villt —
sú rödd, er breytir daufri nótt í dag
og dauðans ópi snýr í vonar-lag?
      Guð er sú rödd.

Hver er sú hönd, sem heldur þessum reyr
um hæstan vetur, svo hann ekki deyr —
sú hönd sem fann, hvar frumkorn lífsins svaf
sem fokstrá, tók það upp og líf því gaf —
sú hönd, er skín á heilagt sólar-hvel,
og hverrar skuggi kallast feikn og hel —
sú hönd, er skrifar lífsins laga-mál
á lilju-blað, sem ódauðlega sál?
      Guð er sú hönd.

PROVIDENCE

Translated by Jakobina Johnson

What is that light, which points the way for me,—
The way where mortal eyes no light can see?
What is that light, on which all light depends
And with creative power through space descends?
What writes of "love" on youth's illumined page
And "life eternal" on the brow of age?
What is thy light, thou fond and cherished Hope,
Without which all the world would darkly grope?
        That light is God.

What is that voice I hear within, through life,
That echoes through our ranks of common strife?—
A father's voice, in wisdom to appraise,
A mother's voice, to comfort all the race.
What voice alone attuned perfection sings,
When all our world of song discordant rings?
Turns into day the darkness of the throng,
And agonies of death to hopeful song?
        That voice is God.

What mighty hand maintained protecting hold
Upon this reed, through direst winter cold?
And found my life, a dormant wind-tossed seed,
And planted it, supplying every need? —
The hand whose torch must touch the sun with light,
Whose shadow means calamity and night.
The hand whose law has written its control
Upon each lily and eternal soul?
        That hand is God.

ÞJÓÐSÖNGUR ÍSLANDS

Eftir Matthías Jochumsson

Ó, guð vors lands, ó, lands vors Guð!
vér lofum þitt heilaga, heilaga nafn.
Úr sólkerfum himnanna hnýta þér krans
þínir herskarar, tímanna safn.
Fyrir þér er einn dagur sem þúsund ár
og þúsund ár dagur, ei meir,
eitt eilífðar smáblóm með titrandi tár,
sem tilbiður guð sinn og deyr.
   Íslands þúsund ár,
eitt eilífðar-smáblóm með titrandi tár,
sem tilbiður guð sinn, og deyr.

Ó, guð! ó, guð! vér föllum fram
og fórnum þér brennandi, brennandi sál,
Guð faðir, vor drottinn frá kyni til kyns
og vér kvökum vort helgasta mál,
vér kvökum og þökkum í þúsund ár,
því þú ert vort einasta skjól;
vér kvökum og þökkum með titrandi tár,
því þú tilbjóst vort forlagahjól.
   Íslands þúsund ár
voru morgunsins húmköldu hrynjandi tár,
sem hitna við skínandi sól.

Ó, guð vors lands! ó, lands vors guð!
vér lifum sem blaktandi, blaktandi strá;
vér deyjum, ef þú ert ei ljós það og líf,
sem að lyftir oss duftinu frá;
ó, ver þú hvern morgun vort ljúfasta líf,
vor leiðtogi í daganna þraut,

THE MILLENNIAL HYMN OF ICELAND

Translated by Jakobina Johnson

Our country's God! Our country's God!
We worship Thy name in its wonder sublime.
The suns of the heavens are set in Thy crown
By Thy legions, the ages of time!
With Thee is each day as a thousand years,
Each thousand of years, but a day.
Eternity's flow'r, with its homage of tears,
That reverently passes away.
    Iceland's thousand years!
Eternity's flow'r, with its homage of tears
That reverently passes away.

Our God, our God, we bow to Thee,
Our spirits most fervent we place in Thy care.
Lord, God of our fathers from age unto age,
We are breathing our holiest prayer.
We pray and we thank Thee a thousand years
For safely protected we stand;
We pray and we bring Thee our homage of tears —
Our destiny rests in Thy hand.
    Iceland's thousand years!
The hoar-frost of morning which tinted those years,
Thy sun rising high, shall command!

Our country's God! Our country's God!
Our life is a feeble and quivering reed;
We perish, deprived of Thy spirit and light
To redeem and uphold in our need.
Inspire us at morn with Thy courage and love,
And lead through the days of our strife!

og á kvöldin vor himneska hvíld og vor hlíf,
og vor hertogi á þjóðlífsins braut.
Íslands þúsund ár
verði gróandi þjóðlíf með þverrandi tár,
sem þroskast á guðsríkisbraut.

EGGERT ÓLAFSSON

Etfir Matthías Jochumsson

Þrútið var loft og þungur sjór,
þokudrungað vor.
Það var hann Eggert Ólafsson,
hann ýtti frá kaldri Skor.

Gamall þulur hjá græði sat,
geigur var svip hans í,
hann mælti við Eggert Ólafsson:
„Mér ógna þau vinda-ský".

„Ég sigli ei skýin, ég sigli sjá!"
svaraði kappinn og hló;
„Ég trúi á guð en grýlur ei
og gleð mig við reiðan sjó".

Gamall þulur frá græði hvarf,
gegndi með þungri lund:
„Þú siglir ei þennan sjó í dag,
þú siglir á guðs þíns fund".

Það var hann Eggert Ólafsson,
hann ýtti frá kaldri Skor,
vindur upp segl og sjálfur við stjórn
settist með formanns þor.

At evening send peace from Thy heaven above,
And safeguard our nation through life.
   Iceland's thousand years!
O, prosper our people, diminish our tears
And guide, in Thy wisdom, through life!

EGGERT ÓLAFSSON
Translated by Skuli Johnson

Dark were the skies, deep groaned the sea,
Fogs dismal the Spring hung o'er,
'Twas he, 'twas Eggert Ólafsson
Who set out from icy Scaur.

Sate by the sea an ancient wight,
With fear was his face o'erspread;
Quoth he to Eggert Ólafsson:
"Yon storm-clouds aloft I dread."

"Clouds sail I not, I sail the sea,"
The hero replied in glee;
"I trust in God but bogies none:
I joy in the angry sea."

Answer then made the ancient wight,
As off from the shore he trod:
"Thou sail'st not o'er this sea today;
Thou sailest to find thy God."

'Twas he, 'twas Eggert Ólafsson
Who set out from icy Scaur;
Sails he drew up and sovran sway
Of helmsman he bravely bore.

Knúðu rastir knerrir tveir,
komið var rok um svið;
síðasti fugl úr fjarri Skor
flögraði' á vinstri hlið.

Á búlkanum situr brúður ung
bleik var hin göfga kinn;
„Ó guð! sú báran er brött og há
hún brotnar í himininn inn!"

„Hækkið þið seglin!" hetjan kvað,
en Helja skjótari varð;
boðinn skall yfir báru-mar
í búlkann var komið skarð.

Það var hann Eggert Ólafsson,
frá unnar-jónum hann stökk
og niður í bráðan Breiðafjörð
í brúðar örmum sökk.

„Það var hann Eggert Ólafsson"
— Íslands vættur kvað —;
„Aldregi græt ég annan meir
en afreks-mennið það".

Ef þrútið er loftið, þungur sjór
og þoku drungað vor,
þú heyrir enn þá harma-ljóð,
sem hljóma frá kaldri Skor.

Burst had the storm, but with boats twain
His arduous course he plied;
A bird that flew from far-off Scaur
Still fluttered on their left side.

Sate on the barge his sweet young bride,
Death-pale turned his lass of love:
"Lord God! That wave is steep and high;
It stretches to heaven above!"

"Hoist high the sails!" the hero cried,
But Doom had more speed than they;
The wave brake o'er the boat-hulks twain
And bore of them much away.

'Twas he, 'twas Eggert Ólafsson
Lo, out of his boat he leapt,
And into blust'ring Broadfirth sank. —
His bride in his arms he kept.

"'Twas he, 'twas Eggert Ólafsson"
Our island's own spirit said,
"Ne'er for another mourn I more
Than this my dear son that's dead."

If skies be dark, deep groan the sea,
And fogs hang the springtide o'er,
You still may hear the wails of woe
That issue from icy Scaur.

KRISTJÁN JÓNSSON
(1842 – 1869)

Kristján Jónsson was born at Krossdal in the North of Iceland. His father, a farmer of very small means, died when the boy was five years old. From the age of fourteen to the age of twenty-two, Jónsson earned his living as a farm-hand. He received only the most elementary education at home, but through his own efforts acquired some knowledge of the Danish, Swedish, English, and German languages and literatures. His poems attracted attention and through the assistance of several generous admirers he entered the College of Iceland in 1864; he attended here until the spring of 1868, but did not graduate. From then until his untimely death he was a private tutor in Vopnafjörður. His poems, Ljóðmæli, have been published four times, — at Reykjavík in 1872, in 1890 and in 1911; and in America (Washington, D. C.) in 1907.

DETTIFOSS

Eftir Kristján Jónsson

Þar sem aldrei á grjóti gráu
gullin mót sólu hlæja blóm
og ginnhvítar öldur gljúfrin háu
grimmefldum nísta heljar-klóm,
kveður þú, foss, minn forni vinur,
með fimbulrómi sí og æ;
undir þér bergið sterka stynur
sem strá í nætur-kulda-blæ.

Kveður þú ljóð um hali horfna
og hetjulíf á fyrri öld;
talar þú margt um frelsið forna
og frægðarinnar dapra kvöld.
Ljósgeislar á þér leika skærir,
liðnir frá sól í gegnum ský;
regnboga-litir titra tærir
tröllauknum bárum þínum í.

Ægilegur og undrafríður
ertu, ið mikla fossa-val;
Aflrammur jafnt þú áfram líður
í eyðilegum hamra-sal.
Tímarnir breytast; bölið sára
það brjóstið slær, er fyrr var glatt;
en alltaf söm þín ógnarbára
ofan um veltist gljúfrið bratt.

Stormarnir hvína, stráin sölna,
stórvaxin alda rís á sæ,
á rjóðum kinnum rósir fölna
í regin-köldum harma-blæ

THE CATARACT

Translated by Runólfur Fjeldsted

No sun-kissed golden-hearted flower
Among the boulders gray can wake;
White billows in terrific power
The cliff with feet of fury shake,
Where thou, old friend, art loud intoning
Forever thy tremendous lay;
Before thy wrath the rocks are groaning,
As reeds in gusts of dying day.

Thy odes arise of heroes vanished
And mighty men of former days;
Thou speakest much of freedom banished
And former fame's departing rays.
Above thee flames a glory gleaming,
That through the clouds comes sifting down,
And rainbow hues resplendent streaming
Thy wild titanic billows crown.

O thou of rolling waters fairest,
Terribly, marvellously fair,
Resistless in thy might thou farest,
Through rocky solitudes and bare;
Things change, for joy's bright fairy dower
Forsakes the woeful heart of flame;
Unbroken bides thy fearful power;
Thou rollest onward just the same.

Hurricanes rise and fall the flowers,
And billows crest above the reef;
Roses of laughing summer showers
Fade in the killing frost of grief;

brennandi tár um bleikan vanga
boga', því hjartað vantar ró —
en alltaf jafnt um æfi langa
aldan í þínu djúpi hló.

Blunda vil ég í bárum þínum,
þá bleikur loksins hníg ég nár,
þar sem að enginn yfir mínu
önduðu líki fellir tár;
og þegar sveit með sorgar-hljóði
syngur döpur of ann'ra ná,
í jörmun-efldum íturmóði
yfir mér skaltu hlæja þá.

GRÖFIN

Eftir Kristján Jónsson

Hvar er í heimi hæli tryggt
og hvíld og mæðu-fró?
Hvar bærist aldrei hjarta hryggt?
Hvar heilög drotnar ró?

Það er in djúpa dauðra gröf,
— þar dvínar sorg og stríð —
er sollin lífs fyrir handan höf
er höfn svo trygg og blíð.

Þú kælir heita hjartans glóð
og heiftar slökkur bál,
þú þaggar niður ástar-óð
og ekkert þekkir tál,

Tears, burning tears on haggard faces
Stream, for the heart can find no peace;
But always on thy current races
In laughters that will never cease.

Deep in thy billows I would slumber,
When at the last my life will fail,
And tears of grief shall none encumber
Over my body still and pale;
When with a dirge and lamentation
Forms may be bowed above a grave,
In mad, terrific exultation
Over me will thy laughters rave.

THE GRAVE

Translated by Gudmund J. Gislason

Where is on earth a safe retreat,
A rest from care and pain?
Where ne'er a grieving heart doth beat
and peace serene doth reign?

It is the deep and silent grave
Where strife and sorrows cease;
Beyond life's dreary ocean wave
A port of rest and peace.

You cool the passions' fiery blaze
And quench the flame of hate;
You hush the yearning lover's lays
And seal the book of fate.

Þú læknar hjartans svöðu-sár
og svæfir auga þreytt,
þú þerrar burtu trega-tár
og trygga hvíld fær veitt.

Þú griðastaður mæðu-manns,
ó, myrka, þögla gröf,
Þú ert ið eina hæli hans
og himins náðargjöf.

TÁRIÐ

Eftir Kristján Jónsson

Þú sæla heimsins svalalind,
ó, silfurskæra tár,
er allri svalar ýta-kind
og ótal læknar sár.

Æ, hverf þú ei af auga mér,
þú ástarblíða tár,
er sorgir heims í burtu ber,
þótt blæði hjartans sár.

Mér himneskt ljós í hjarta skín
í hvert sinn er ég græt,
en drottinn telur tárin mín —
ég trúi' og huggast læt.

You heal the broken heart forlorn,
And close the eyes oppressed;
You dry the tears of anguish born
— Oh blessed place of rest.

To one distressed a refuge sweet
Oh dark and silent grave;
You are the only sure retreat
That heaven's mercy gave.

THE TEAR

Translated by Jakobina Johnson

A blessed cooling fount thou art,
O gleaming pearly tear;
Refreshing every human heart —
A balm where wounds appear.

Oh leave me not when grief holds sway,
Thou tender friend in need.
Thus human woes are borne away,
Though wounded hearts must bleed.

I weep and feel my hopes restored,
— A light from heaven I see.
My tears are numbered by the Lord,
My faith shall comfort me.

JÓN ÓLAFSSON
(1850—1916)

Jón Ólafsson was born at Kolfreyjustaður in the East of Iceland, where his father was then a clergyman. He was a brother of Páll Ólafsson (see above). Jón Ólafsson was a student in the College of Iceland from 1863 to 1869. At a very early age he became interested in literary work and politics. This interest he retained through life. He was an ardent and outspoken lover of freedom; in fact, he twice had to leave his native land because of his frank political utterances. The greater part of his life he was engaged in journalism, either in Iceland or in America. For a number of years he was a member of the Icelandic Parliament. He wrote much on various subjects. His poems, Söngvar og kvæði (Songs and poems), appeared in 1877; a second enlarged edition, in 1892; and a third enlarged edition, in 1896.

KÓNGSRÍKIÐ MITT

Eftir Jón Ólafsson

Dregur upp skyflóka' og dimmir í geimi
dapurt og kaldlegt er útlit í heimi.
En ég á mér kóngsríki, fimbulvítt, fáð,
fagurt og sólheiðríkt draumanna láð.

Seint kemur vorið og seint laufgast eikur,
seint grænkar þettað ár völlurinn bleikur;
en eilíft er vor og sígrænt að sjá
sólríku draumlandi fegurðar á.

Af fósturjörð hrakinn ég fæ ei að líta
föðurland síþráð með tindana hvíta;
en fósturland á ég mér andans í geim
Íslandi fegra í draumanna heim.

Þó að í prísund mig dómarinn dæmi
og Danskurinn burtu frá ættjörð mig flæmi,
hér á ég frístað; þeir hrakið ei fá
himnesku draumanna landi mig frá.

Vinum og ættingjum frá hlaut ég flýja,
framandi og einmana í landinu nýja;
en andi minn dvelur þó einatt þeim hjá
indælu draumlandi hugarins á.

MY KINGDOM

Translated by Vilhjalmur Stefansson

The land is in gloom and the cloud-banks have risen
To blot out the world from the field of my vision;
But the June sun still sparkles on shimmering streams
In a land fair and cloudless — my Kingdom of Dreams.

Spring is slow in its coming; the bare trees still shiver;
Not for weeks will the dew on the young grasses
                                         quiver;
But the spring is eternal, the white petal gleams
With the dew of the morn, in the land of my dreams.

An exile, I pine for the heaven-blue fountains
Of my island-home's snow-capped and green-
                          bosomed mountains;
But a land even fairer than it you will see
If you come over seas to my dreamland with me.

Though to prison the courts of our lords may con-
                              sign me,
Though the Danes may exile and their puppets
                              malign me,
I know an asylum where all men are free,
And my cottage stands waiting in dreamland for me.

My exile left friends that I loved far behind me,
And a stranger I am in the land Fate assigned me;
But my spirit still dwells with the loved ones at home,
In my dreams I am with them, wherever I roam.

Ýmsa þá kærustu' af ástvinum mínum
ískalt nú grafarhúm felur mér sýnum;
en nær sem ég vil fer ég samt þá að sjá
sólheiðu draumlandi minningar á.

Fátækur veraldar er ég af auði;
á ei til morguns af daglegu brauði.
En hvað hirði' ég gullsins um glitrandi sand?
Gangmynt er kærleiki' um draumanna land!

Hvað eru konungar heims þessa', að kalla?
Hásætið veltur þá minnst varir alla.
Um konungdóm þeirra mig kæri' ég ei grand.—
Kóngsríkið mitt það er draumanna land!

Og sárt þegar hugraunir hjartanu svíða
og heimur mig grætir og þungt er að líða,
kyssir mér tárin af brennheitri brá
brosfögur draumlandsins vonarsól þá.

Loks þegar endað ég lífsins hef daga,
loks þegar ormarnir hold þetta naga —
bænheyr mig, drottinn, ég bið um að fá
byggja með ástvinum draumland mitt þá!

Some that I cherished the darkness has hidden
Where even the entrance of love is forbidden;
I cannot go to them, but still they are free
To walk through the meadows of dreamland with me.

Riches I have not, but why should I sorrow
Though poverty oft have no bread for the morrow?
My way is not nearly so hard as it seems
For fancy is gold in the land of my dreams.

What are the kings of the earth in their splendor?
Their thrones topple down on their vanishing grandeur.
For their courts and their scepters I care not at all;
In the kingdoms of dreamland the thrones never fall.

In the dark night of sorrow, when heart-strings are
                                        breaking
And no balm of this world soothes the pain and the
                                        aching,
The soft dawn of dreamland may bring on the day
And the sunshine of hope kiss the tear-drops away.

When my voyage is ended on life's tossing billow,
When at last in the evening my head seeks the pillow,
Then God, hear my prayer, for this it will be:
"Let the friends that I love dwell in dreamland
                                        with me!"

GESTUR PÁLSSON
(1852—1891)

Gestur Pálsson was born at Miðhús in Reykhólasveit in the
West of Iceland. He was the son of a farmer. After graduating
from the College of Iceland in 1875, Pálsson entered upon the
study of theology at the University of Copenhagen, but soon
became more interested in literature. He became a great ad-
mirer of George Brandes and was deeply influenced by his
realism. In 1882 Pálsson returned to Reykjavík, where he was
for some years engaged in journalism. In 1890 he emigrated to
Winnipeg, Canada, and became editor of the weekly Heimskringla; but he died the following year. He is primarily re-
membered as a short-story writer, but he also wrote some poetry of merit. His writings, prose and poetry, were published
in Reykjavík in 1902 [and in Winnipeg in the same year. A
new edition of his works appeared in Reykjavík in 1927.

BETLIKERLINGIN

Eftir Gest Pálsson

Hún hokin sat á tröppu,
       en hörkufrost var á,
og hnipraði sig saman,
       unz í kuðung hún lá,
og kræklóttar hendurnar
       titra til og frá,
um tötrana að fálma,
       sér velgju til að ná.

Og augað var svo sljótt,
       sem þess sloknað hefði ljós
í stormbylnum tryllta,
       um lífsins voða-ós
það hvarflaði glápandi,
       stefnulaust og stirt,
og staðnæmdist við ekkert —
       svo örvæntingarmyrkt.

Á enni sátu rákir
       og hrukka hrukku sleit,
þær heljarrúnir sorgar,
       sem enginn þýða veit;
hver skýra kann frá prísund
       og plágum öllum þeim.
sem píslarvottar gæfunnar
       liða hér í heim?

Hún var kannske perla,
       sem týnd í tímans haf
var töpuð og glötuð,
       svo enginn vissi af,
eða gimsteinn sem forðum
       var greyptur láns í baug,
en glerbrot var hún orðin
       á mannfélagsins haug.

THE BEGGAR WOMAN

Translated by Skuli Johnson

She cringed and stooped nigh steps
        when the winter frost controlled;
She huddled her together
        and to a snail-shape rolled;
With her gnarled hands she groped e'er,
        atrembling, to and fro,
And at her tatters clutched she
        that they might warmth bestow.

Her eyes were dull, precisely
        as if their glow had gone
To Death amid the storms dread
        that rage Life's sea upon;
They — straying, staring, aimless
        in motion, well-nigh stark,
Ne'er staying on an object
        with deep despair were dark.

Upon her forehead, wrinkles
        and furrows many sate —
The dreadful Runes of Sorrow
        that no man may translate:
By whom can all the trials
        and troubles be unfurled
That souls who're Fortune's martyrs
        must suffer in this world?

Perhaps she was a pearl pure
        that was 'neath Time's sea tossed
And so beyond all ken
        was thus ever wholly lost;
Or else she was a gem,
        erst enringed in fortune's keep:
There lay she now — a glasspiece
        upon Earth's refuse-heap.

ÞORSTEINN ERLINGSSON
(1858—1914)

Þorsteinn Erlingsson was born at Stórumörk in the South of Iceland. He was graduated from the College of Iceland in 1883. He spent some years in study at the University of Copenhagen. In 1895 he returned to Iceland where he was for several years engaged in journalism. From 1902 until his death he resided in Reykjavík, earning his living primarily by private tutoring. During his later years he received a small stipend from the Icelandic government for his literary work. He wrote a number of essays and articles. His first volume of poems, Þyrnar (Thorns), appeared in 1897; a second enlarged edition, in 1905; and a third enlarged edition, in 1918. In 1913 the first part of Erlingsson's significant narrative poem, Eiðurinn (The Oath), appeared; this, however, he never completed. A second edition was published in 1925.

ARFURINN

Eftir Þorstein Erlingsson

Þú átt kannske frækna og fengsæla þjóð,
þér finnst kannske ólga þitt göfuga blóð,
er sástu' hana sigurför halda,
þar nábúinn fátæki fjötraður sat,
sem föðurleifð varði á meðan hann gat,
er látinn var liðsmunar gjalda.

Þá ljómar um salina þjóðheiður þinn,
er þrekaði bandinginn leiddur er inn,
og þá er þér sigurinn sætur;
og veizlan í höllinni veglegri þá
og vínið þar bjartara skálunum á,
ef einhver er inni sem grætur.

En þú, sem að hefur í hjartanu blóð,
úr hrakinni, smáðri og kúgaðri þjóð,
og eitrað á hörmungar árum:
Það knýr þig svo fast, þegar arfurinn er
á einverustundunum réttur að þér
af minningum mörgum og sárum.

Þó holdið á örmunum þrútnaði þar,
sem þrælkaði faðirinn hlekkina bar;
Það harkaði' hann af sér í hljóði. —
En kvölin, sem nísti' hann, er nakinn hann lá
og níðingahnúarnir gengu' honum á:
hún brennur í sonarins blóði.

THE HERITAGE

Translated by Vilhjalmur Stefansson

It may be that yours is a powerful land;
It may be your heart swells with pride where you stand
When her armies come home from afar
With the man who has fought for his home while
                          his strength
Could support him, but now has been conquered
                             at length
Bound fast to your triumphal car.

Your fatherland's glory illumines the halls
When, loaded with fetters, the prissoner falls
On the threshold. Your triumph is sweet,
For you feel, at the banquet the gloom of his soul
Will brighten the shimmer of wine in the bowl
And lighten the tripping of feet.

But for you through whose heart surges blood
                        from the veins
Of a people downtrodden and loaded with chains,
A nation that all men despise,
The trial is bitter when Memory's hand
Leads your soul through the barren and desolate land
And naught but your shame meets your eyes.

When the chains that he bore made the muscles to swell,
And the sting of the lash brought the blood drops that fell
Where the father that cherished you stood,
The anguish that quivered and shot through his frame
Brought neither a cry nor a word; but the shame
Now simmers and burns in your blood.

SKILMÁLARNIR

Eftir Þorstein Erlingsson

Ef þér ei ægir allra djöfla
      upphlaup að sjá,
og hverri tign að velli velt,
      sem veröldin á,
og höggna sundur hverja stoð,
      sem himnana ber;
þá skal ég syngja sönginn minn
      og sitja hjá þér.

Og ef þú hatar herra þann,
      sem harðfjötrar þig,
og kúgar til að elska ekkert
      annað en sig,
en kaupir hrós af hræddum þrælum.
      hvar sem hann fer,
þá skal ég líka af heilum huga
      hata með þér.

Ef anntu þeim, sem heftur hlær
      og hristir sín bönd,
og vildi ekki krjúpa og kyssa
      á kúgarans hönd,
en hugum-stór að hinzta dómi
      hlekkina ber;
þá skal ég eins af öllu hjarta
      unna með þér.

Og ef þig langar leyndardóma
      lífsins að sjá,
og biðjirðu um þess Barnagull
      og byrjir á „á"

THE TERMS

Translated by Jakobina Johnson

If seeing all the fiends rebel,
      won't smite you with fear,
And every dignitary crushed,
      tradition holds dear;
And every pillar of the heavens
      cloven in two; —
— Then I shall calmly sing my song
      while sitting with you.

And if you hate the tyrant
      who would shackle your feet,
And all your homage claims to make
      his victory complete,
While buying praise from cringing slaves
      who fawn at his shoe, —
— Then I shall proudly join in that
      hatred with you.

And if you love the prisoner
      whose courage remains,
Who will not kneel and kiss the hand
      that placed him in chains,
But dauntless, till the final judgment
      carries them through,
— Sincerely, with my heart and soul,
      I'll love him with you.

And if you wish the secret lore
      of nature to read,
Approaching it in meekness,
      like a child in its need,

og lest þar ekkert öfugt
  gegnum annnarra gler;
þá vil ég feginn líka læra
  að lesa með þér.

Ef þú ert fús að halda á haf,
  þó hrönnin sé óð,
og hefir enga ábyrgð keypt
  í eilífðarsjóð,
en lætur bátinn bruna djarft
  um boða og sker,
þá skal ég sæll um sjóinn allan
  sigla með þér.

Og seinast þegar svarta nóttin
  sígur á lönd,
og dökkar hrannir hrynja um knör
  og hvergi sér strönd,
þá láttu bátinn horfi halda,
  hvert sem hann ber:
og ég skal sæll á svarta djúpið
  sigla með þér.

SÓLSKRÍKJAN
Eftir Þorstein Erlingsson

Sú rödd var svo fögur, svo hugljúf og hrein,
sem hljómaði til mín úr dálitlum runni;
hún sat þar um nætur og söng þar á grein
svo sólfögur ljóð um svo margt, sem ég unni,
og kvöld eftir kvöld hóf hún ástarljóð ein —
ó, ef að þú vissir, hvað mikið hún kunni.

Accepting nothing twisted
          through another man's view,
— Then humbly I'll begin at the
          beginning with you.

And if you dare to sail midst crushing
          ice-floes at play
— With no eternal safety bonds,
          insuring your day, —
But speed the vessel bravely
          with these perils in view,
— Then gladly all the Seven Seas
          I'll voyage with you.

And when the final night of nights
          descends on the shore,
And inky waves envelop us,
          and land is no more —
— If, when we drift, you grasp the helm,
          with firm hand and true,
Content, upon that unknown deep,
          I'll venture with you.

THE SHRIKE
Translated by Runólfur Fjeldsted

Her voice was so charming, so heart-felt and clear,
That rose, from the little copse, thrilling and ringing.
Her notes were of things most beloved and dear:
A sunburst of song through the night-shadows flinging.
And sweet every eve were her love-lays to hear.
O, if you could guess at the wealth of her singing.

Hún kvað um sitt fjölbreytta fjalldala skraut,
hve frítt er og rólegt að eiga þar heima,
hve mjúkt er í júní í ljósgrænni laut,
hve létt þar er vetrarins hörmum að gleyma,
og hvað þá er inndælt við ættjarðarskaut
um ástir og vonir að syngja og dreyma.

En sætust af öllum og sigrandi blíð
hún söng mér þar ljóðin um dalbúans næði,
um lundinn sinn kæra og lynggróna hlíð,
þó lítil og fátækleg væru þau bæði;
en svipurinn hýrnar, þér sýnast þau fríð
í syngjandi snjótitlings vornæturkvæði.

Þar söng hún í kyrrðinni elskhugans óð
um óbyggðar heiðar og víðsýnið fríða,
og æskunnar barnglaða, blíðróma ljóð,
sem biður þess sumarið aldrei að líða;
því sitja þar vorkvöldin hlustandi hljóð,
því hika þar nætur og dreymandi bíða.

En fjarri' er nú söngur þinn, sólskríkjan mín,
og sumur þíns vinar hin fegurstu liðin;
hann langar svo oft heim á Þórsmörk til þín,
hann þráir svo ljóðin og vornæturfriðinn, —
hann harmar í skógunum hrjósturlönd sín,
hann hlustar sem gestur á náttgalakliðinn.

Her lays were of peace in her mountain-dale home,
Its manifold beauty in summertide gleaming;
How radiant June in the dells loves to roam;
How sorrows of winter are lost in her beaming.
How wonderful then, in the isle o'er the foam,
Of hope and of love to be singing and dreaming.

She sang, in her softest and mellowest air,
The peace undisturbed of the croft that lay nether;
Her heathery slope and her bower so fair,
Though humble and commonplace were both together;
A charm kindles all, and they seem rich and rare,
When low pipes the snow-bird in balmy spring-
       weather.

She sang in the stillness the lover's fond lay,
Of heath-moors and prospect so glorious ever;
Of infancy's happiest, tenderest day,
That prays to the summer to bide there forever;
There evenings in listening silence must stay.
There loiter the nights, nor thy dream-bond dissever.

Dear songster, thy notes are afar off from me,
Thy friend's brightest summers have all now departed;
So often he longs for his homeland and thee.
He yearns for the spring and thy lays music-hearted.
He loves in the forest his mountain-heaths free,
And nightingale's charm not the least so has smarted.

KVÖLD

Eftir Þorstein Erlingsson

Nú blika við sólarlag sædjúpin köld;
ó, svona' ætti að vera hvert einasta kvöld,
með hreinan og ljúfan og heilnæman blæ
og himininn bláan og speglandi sæ.

Ó, ástblíða stund, þú ert unaðssæl mér,
því allt er svo ljómandi fagurt hjá þér,
og hafið hið kalda svo hlýlegt og frítt,
og hrjóstruga landið mitt vinlegt og blítt.

Og fjallhnúkaraðirnar rísa í kring,
sem risar á verði við sjóndeildarhring;
og kvöldroðinn brosfagur boðar þar drótt
hinn blíðasta dag eftir ljúfustu nótt.

HREIÐRIÐ MITT

Eftir Þorsfein Erlingsson

Þér frjálst er að sjá, hve ég bólið mitt bjó,
ef börnin mín smáu þú lætur í ró;
þú manst að þau eiga sér móður;
og ef að þau lifa þau syngja þér söng
um sumarið blíða og vorkvöldin löng —
Þú gerir það, vinur minn góður.

EVENING

Translated by Jakobina Johnson

The gold of the sunset illumines the deep.
O, thus should each evening prepare me for sleep;
A soft, cooling breeze with the freshness of dew.
— The ocean a mirror of heavenly blue.

Thou sweetest of moments, I'm charmed by thy spell,
Composure and beauty enthroned with thee dwell.
The cold changeful ocean looks friendly and mild,
— My own rugged country now smiles on its child.

The mountain-peaks towering stately around
Are giants on guard where the sky meets the ground.
This sunset foretells that the day shall be bright,
That follows the steps of this wonderful night.

MY NEST

Translated by Gudmund J. Gislason

Your're welcome to see how I built my nest,
If my babies dear you will not molest —
Remember that they have a mother;
And if they live, to you songs they'll sing
About summer fair and the nights of spring;
So treat them, my friend, like a brother.

EINAR HJÖRLEIFSSON KVARAN
(b. 1859)

Einar Hjörleifsson Kvaran was born at Goðdalir in the North of Iceland. He was graduated from the College of Iceland in 1881. He then studied at the University of Copenhagen for some years. In 1885 he emigrated to America. For ten years he remained in Winnipeg, Canada, the greater part of the time as editor of the weekly Lögberg. At the end of that period he returned to Iceland, and was associated, in an editorial capacity, with various Icelandic publications until 1909. Since then he has devoted his time mostly to literary work, for which he receives an annual stipend from the Icelandic government. He has been editor of Mergunn (Morning), the official organ of Icelandic spiritualists, since 1920. Kvaran is one of Iceland's foremost novelists and short-story writers. He has also published a great number of essays, articles, and reviews in various periodicals. His poems, Ljóðmæli, appeared in 1893.

MINNI VESTURHEIMS

Eftir Einar Hjörleifsson Kvaran

Önnur lönd með ellifrægð sig skreyta,
æva-löngu dauðum kappafans,
út í dimma fornöld lýsa' og leita
lífsins perlum að og heiðurs-krans.
Þú ert landið þess er dáð vill drýgja,
dýpst og sterkast kveður lífsins brag.
Þú ert land hins þróttarmikla' og nýja.
Þú varst aldrei fegri en nú — í dag.

Önnur lönd í kóngadýrð sig dúða,
dýrast meta fágað líf í sal.
Hér er starfið skærara' öllum skrúða
skýrast aðalsmerki snót og hal,
Hér er frelsið lífsins ljúfust sunna,
líka fólksins öruggasta band.
Allir þeir, sem frelsi framast unna
fyrst af öllu horfa, á þetta land.

Vesturheimur, veruleikans álfa,
vonarland hins unga, sterka manns,
fyll þú móð og manndáð okkur sjálfa
móti hverjum óvin sannleikans;
lyft oss yfir agg og þrætudíki
upp á sólrík háfjöll kærleikans.
Vesturheimur, veruleikans ríki,
vonarland hins unga, sterka manns.

THE WESTLAND (AMERICA)

Translated by Skuli Johnson

While other lands with ancient fame them dower
And deck them with their hero-hosts long dead,
And deem they find life's blessings in the bower
Of ages flown if o'er them light is shed,
Thou art the land of those who choose the rigour
Of doughty deeds and best attune Life's Lay,
Thou art the land of youthfulness and vigour
And never wert more famous than today.

While other lands them deck with regal glory
And judge supreme the genteel palace-life,
Here work outshines all show enshrined in story
And stamps as noble all who share its strife.
Here Liberty is loved like sunlight fairest
And is our surest unifying band,
And all who feel that Freedom is man's rarest
Gift, first direct their gaze toward this land.

Great western world! Reality's new nation!
The Realm of Hope for all the young and strong!
Fill us with courage and high aspiration
'Gainst every foe that aims the Truth to wrong.
From Wrangling's Fenlands waft us on fleet pinions
Until we rest Love's sun-lit heights among.
Great Western World! Reality's Dominion!
The Realm of Hope for all the young and strong!

KOSSINN

Eftir Einar Hjörleifsson Kvaran

Í hug hans var sólskin og hjartað var ungt,
þá heim kom hún til hans — Sorgin.
Og fótatak hennar fannst honum þungt
sem fallandi hamraborgin.

Himininn társtraumum hellti' út um lönd.
Á húsþaki vindurinn stundi.
Og Sorgin rétti' honum svellkalda hönd.
Hann seint mun gleyma þeim fundi.

Hún leiddi' hann út yfir firnindi og fjöll
með fárköldum jökulbogum,
og út yfir þyrnum alþakinn völl
og eldvötn með glóandi logum.

Þau komu loks út í koldimman skóg.
Þar kyssti' hún hann líkt og í draumi.
Svo leið hún á burt í léttri ró
sem laufblað í þungum straumi.

En hvert sem forlögin flytja þann mann,
um fjöll eða sæ eða torgin —
hann kennir á enni sér kossinn þann,
er kyssti' hún hann forðum, Sorgin.

THE KISS

Translated by Runólfur Fjeldsted

His day was all sunshine, his young heart was gay,
When she came — the Lady of Sorrow.
He feared that a weight, when her steps turned his way,
Like mountains would fall on the morrow.

The clouds rained a tempest of tears o'er the land,
The winds were complaining and calling,
And she came and put forth her heart-chilling hand —
O, that was a moment appalling.

She led him by wild wastes and mountains that frowned
With chilling and frost-bitten spires,
And where thorns with agony covered the ground,
And lakes that were raging with fires.

She kissed him, when time like a trance on him lay,
Where loomed sunless forests aquiver,
Then quietly, lightly, she floated away,
As leaves on a soundless river.

Wherever he wanders by sea or by shore,
Whatever his lot on the morrow,
His brow ever burns with the kiss, that of yore
She kissed him — the Lady of Sorrow.

HANNES HAFSTEIN
(1861—1922)

Hannes Pétursson Hafstein was born at Möðruvellir in the
North of Iceland. He was graduated from the College of Iceland in 1880, and received his law degree (candidatus juris)
from the University of Copenhagen in 1886. He held many
public offices and became one of the leading statesmen of his
day. He was minister (ráðherra) for Iceland, the first Icelander
to hold that office, from 1904 to 1909, and again from 1912
to 1914. He was also for a number of years a member of the
Icelandic parliament (the Althing). The greater part of Hafstein's poetry is the product of his earlier years, although he
retained throughout life his literary interest. His first volume, Ýmisleg ljóðmæli (Various poems), appeared in
1893; a collected edition was published in 1916, and again
in 1925.

VIÐ VALAGILSÁ

Eftir Hannes Hafstein

Hefur þú verið hjá Valagilsá
um vordag í sólheitri blíðu?
Kolmórauð, freyðandi þeytist hún þá,
og þokar fram stórbjörgum gilinu frá,
sem kastast í ólgandi straumfalli stríðu.
Orgar í boðum, en urgar í grjóti,
engu er stætt í því dynjandi róti.
Áin, sem stundum er ekki í hné,
er orðin að skaðræðisfljóti.

Hefur þú gengið að gilinu þá
til gamans, á meðan þú bíður?
Því fyrst eftir miðnættið minnkar á,
og meðan er skemmtun gljúfrið að sjá,
hve grenjandi hrönnin við hrikaberg sýður.
Hanga þar skuggar á hroðaklettum
hengdir draugar með svipum grettum.
Standberg við standberg þar hreykjast upp há,
með hamrasvip, fettum og brettum.

Kom þú í gilið, en haf eigi hátt,
þeir í hömrunum þola það eigi.
Verði þér hlátur, þá heyrir þú brátt
þeir hljóða svo dimman úr hverri átt,
Þeir vilja að allt, nema áin, þegi,
Þeir eru einvaldir í því gili,
ótal búa í svörtu þili,
gnísta tönnum við barinn botn
og byltast í grænum hyli.

*   *   *

VALAGILS-RIVER

Translated by Gudmund J. Gislason

Have you ever been on a warm sunny day
In springtime at Valagils river?
Dashing on madly and sputtering spray,
It loosens great rocks from the gorge in its way,
And swirls them about till they crash and quiver.
Billows are howling and boulders are clashing,
Nothing withstands the wild current's fierce lashing.
Stream which at times would not reach to your knee
Is torrent all barriers smashing.

Have you then strolled thru the canyon grey
For enjoyment, while you were waiting?
You can not more pleasantly pass away
The time until midnight and then you may
Expect to behold the mad torrent abating.
Shadowy forms to the cliffs are clinging —
Eerie specters from gallows swinging.
Rock columns sphinx-like with visages grim,
In row upon row there are stringing.

Come thru the canyon, but speak not for fear
They in the cliffs can not bear your voices.
Should you but laugh you would suddenly hear
Them roaring so gruffly from far and near;
They tolerate none but the river's noises.
They are supreme in this canyon, beware,
and dwell in these rock-walls everywhere,
Gnash their teeth in a ghostly play
And roll in the green abyss there.

*   *   *

Nú er loks komin nætur stund,
og nú sýnist árvatnið blárra.
Drýpur af stráum og döggvot er grund.
Mig dreymdi, að nú væri skárra.
Hestarnir híma' upp á völlum.
Gljúfrið er draugslega dimmt,
og drungasorti á fjöllum.

Straumur freyðir og stekkur hátt,
steinar í botni skarka,
sogar strengur og suðar kátt.
En — samt held ég láti nú slarka.
Ég ætla að sjá hvað setur,
hvort sjóðandi straumiðufall
eða brjóstþrekinn klár hefur betur.

SKARPHÉÐINN Í BRENNUNNI.

Eftir Hannes Hafstein

Buldi við brestur,
brotnaði þekjan.
Reið niður rjáfur
og rammir ásar.

Skall yfir eldhafið ólgandi, logandi,
eldvargar runnu fram hvæsandi, sogandi,
reykurinn glóðþrunginn gaus upp úr kafinu,
gaflaðið eitt stóð sem klettur úr hafinu.

Nár var þá Njáll,
nár var Bergþóra.
Burtu var Kári,
brunninn Grímur,

At last 'tis night upon the view,
The river is seemingly clearer.
Wet is the herbage and dripping with dew.
I dreamed that my going was nearer.
The horses are huddled together,
The canyon is eerie and dark,
And dreary the mountain weather.

Foaming eddies are leaping high,
Stones on their rockbed clatter,
Gaily rapids go roaring by,
Yet — I'll risk how hard they can batter.
I'll see without waiting longer,
If turbulent torrent amuck
Or my sinewy steed is the stronger.

SKARPHEDINN AMONG THE FLAMES

Translated by Gudmund J. Gislason

Booming and quaking,
Cracking and breaking,
Down crashed the rafters
And roofbeams sturdy.
Torrent of flames burst forth seething and vicious,
On rushed the fire-demons, raging, malicious.
Smoke-columns blazing rose up from the holocaust.
The gable alone stood like rock in an ocean vast.

Then both were dead
Njall and Bergthora.
Gone was Kari,
Cremated Grimur,

höggvinn Helgi.
Héðinn stóð einn
tepptur við gaflað
og glotti við tönn.

Gulrauðar glóðir
glampa og braka,
blóðroðin birta
blaktir um garpinn.

Skín hún á andlitið skarpfölt og tannirnar,
skiptandi blæ, meðan eldsloga hrannirnar
flétta úr eldtungum umgjörðir titrandi
utanum hetjuna, bjartar og glitrandi.

Hélt hann á rammri
Rimmugýgi.
„Hvað er nú, öx mín!
hitnar þér nokkuð?
Þú skyldir þeygi
svo þurrmynnt vera,
væri í annað
en eld að bíta".

Gunnspár þá glóði
geisli á blaði,
stirndi á stál
og stæltar eggjar.

Skarphéðinn glotti við skínandi stálinu:
„Skil ég þig, öx mín, ber kveðjur úr bálinu".
Hefndþrungna bengýgi hóf hann og lét 'ana
hverfa í gaflaðið, langt upp á fetana.

Hewn down Helgi.
Hedinn remained
Pinned at the gable
And scornfully grinned.

Orange-red embers
Glisten and crackle.
Blood-tinted lightbeams
Play on the hero.

They shine on his teeth and pale sharp-featured
                                    countenance,
Changing in hue, while the blaze billows leap and dance,
Twisting from firetongues a flamewreath all flittering,
Encircling the warrior, brilliantly glittering.

His hands were holding
Battle-Ogre.
"How art thou, my ax!
Heating somewhat?
Thou wouldst not be
So blue and arid
were there aught else
Than flames to sunder".

Red-rays prophetic
Of future blood sheds,
Glowed on the ax-head's
Trenchant edges.

Skarphedinn grinned at the shining steel: "I know thee
Ax of mine, out from the flames bring regards from me".
Swinging the vengeance-filled weapon with power he
Buried it deep in the core of the gable-tree.

Leit hann á eldbranda
aðfallandi.
Hvað var í huga
Höskuldsbana?
Kominn bónleiður
til búðar hinztu,
eldibrand tók sér
í axar stað

Aleinn örlögum
ofurseldur
horfðist í augu
við eld og dauða.

Færðust að logarnir, brennandi, brakandi,
báldrekar skriðu fram, eldhausa skakandi,
lögðust að fótum hans, fæturna sleikjandi
flakandi tungum, og glóðmökkum hreykjandi.

Hnykluðust vöðvar
á herðum þreknum,
efldum er armi
upp hann lyfti;
losaði kyrtil
frá loðnu brjósti,
brenndi sér helrún:
inn helga kross.

Beit svo á kampinn og krosslagði armana,
karlmennskuró sló um ennið og hvarmana.
Ljómandi kring um hann logarnir kvikuðu,
ljósgeislar fagnandi á honum blikuðu.

*   *   *

He looked at burning brands
Falling about him:
What was in the mind
Of Höskuld's slayer?
Weary combatant
At his journey's end
Grasped a firebrand
In the axe's stead.

Alone, a victim
Of fate most dire
Stood face to face
With fire and death.

Flames moved up toward him, crackling and lowering,
Fire dragons crawled round him, glowing sparks
                                        showering,
Crouched at his feet awhile, licking them cowering
With tongues a-flaring, then mounted up towering.

Muscles grew tense
On robust shoulders
As he raised his arm
Surcharged with vigor,
Uncovered his hairy
Chest and upon it
Seared, as his death-rune,
The holy cross.

Biting his beard, and his arms folding tacitly,
Valorous calm settled over him placidly,
Brilliant round him the flames swept a-flittering,
Lightbeams triumphantly played on him, glittering.

*   *   *

Dimmt er í skála,
dökkir mekkir
hefjast úr ösku
og hrundum rústum.
Inni við gaflað
í ösku stendur
Héðinn örendur
með opnum sjónum.
Heyrst ei hafði
hósti né stunur.

STORMUR

Eftir Hannes Hafstein

Ég elska þig, stormur, sem geisar um grund
og gleðiþyt vekur í blaðstyrkum lund,
en gráfeysknu kvistina bugar og brýtur
og bjarkirnar treystir um leið og þú þýtur.

Þú skefur burt fannir af foldu og hól,
þú feykir burt skýjum frá ylbjartri sól,
og neistann upp blæs þú og bálar upp loga,
og bryddir með litskrúði úthöf og voga.

Þú þenur út seglin og byrðinginn ber
og birtandi, andhreinn um jörðina fer;
þú loftilla, dáðlausa lognmollu hrekur
og lífsanda starfandi hvarvetna vekur.

Og þegar þú sigrandi' um foldina fer,
þá finn ég að þrótturinn eflist í mér.
Ég elska þig kraftur, sem öldurnar reisir,
ég elska þig máttur, sem þokuna leysir.

Dim is the cabin,
Dark smoke-columns
Rise from the ruins
And reeking embers.
Close by the gable
In the ashes stands
Skarphedinn dead
With open eyes.
There had not been heard
A cough or a moan.

THE STORM
Translated by Skuli Johnson

I love thee, O Storm o'er the wold that dost sweep,
And waken'st glad flutters in woodlands asleep;
The gray, withered branches thou breakest and triest
The birch-boles' endurance, as by them thou fliest.

Thou waftest the snowdrifts from vale and from height
And clearest the clouds from the sun out of sight;
And sparks thou arousest and fires thou fannest;
The bays and the sea with waves sparkling thou
spannest.

Thou fillest the sails, and the ships thou dost bear,
And light-giving, cleansing, o'er Earth dost thou fare;
But foul-aired and indolent calm thou pursuest
And everywhere Life's breath and vigour renewest.

When thou in thy triumph dost wend o'er the lea
I feel that new vigour arises in me;
I love thee, great might in the wild waves indwelling,
I love thee, great might, the dank fog-hosts dispelling.

Ég elska þig, elska þig, eilífa stríð,
með ólgandi blóði þér söng minn ég býð.
Þú alfrjálsi loftfari, hamast þú hraður;
hugur minn fylgir þér djarfur og glaður.

UNDIR KALDADAL

Eftir Hannes Hafstein

Ég vildi óska það yrði nú regn
eða þá bylur á Kaldadal,
og ærlegur kaldsvali okkur gegn
ofan úr háreistum jöklasal

Loft við þurfum. Við þurfum það,
að þvo burt dáðleysis mollukóf,
þurfum að koma á kaldan stað,
í karlmennsku vorri halda próf.

Þurfum stað, þar sem stormur hvín
og steypiregn gerir hörund vott.
Þeir geta þá skolfið og skammazt sín
sem skjálfa vilja. Þeim er það gott.

Ef kaldur stormur um karlmann ber
og kinnar bítur og reynir fót,
þá finnur 'ann hitann í sjálfum sér
og sjálfs sín kraft til að standa mót.

Að kljúfa rjúkandi kalda gegn
það kætir hjartað í vöskum hal. —
Ég vildi það yrði nú ærlegt regn
og íslenzkur stormur á Kaldadal.

I love, Storm, thy striving forever and aye;
Thou stirrest my blood, thee I offer my lay.
Fly, fly thou unfettered, through air-haunts onfaring:
I'll follow thy guidance with joy and daring.

NEARING COLD-DALE

Translated by Jakobina Johnson

I wish for rain — and I wish for snow,
As on through Cold-Dale our horses glide;
And that a bracing wind may blow
Down from the glacial mountain-side.

We need the air, and we need the bath,
To cleanse our spirits of slothful rest.
We need the lash of an ice wind's wrath
Of manly courage a fitting test.

We need a ride where the wild winds wake
And the rain beats down in relentless mood,
That they may humbly shiver and shake
Who shiver must. It may do them good.

When a noble storm meets a manly man
— The face must tingle and foot must tire —
It draws on his latent strength to fan
The glowing coals of a hidden fire.

To brave the tempest with might and main
Lends steel to courage and spurs to pride.
— I hope there vill be a rush of rain
Or an Iceland storm — on our Cold-Dale ride.

EINAR BENEDIKTSSON
(b. 1864)

Einar Benediktsson was born at Elliðavatn in the South o
Iceland. He is the son of Benedikt Sveinsson, a noted political
leader. Benediktsson was graduated from the College of Iceland in 1884. He received his law degree from the University
of Copenhagen in 1892. He has held public offices in Iceland
and also interested himself in politics and journalism. Since
1907 he has, however, for the most part lived outside of Iceland, and has travelled extensively. His principal works are
the following: Sögur og kvæði (Stories and poems), 1897;
Hafblik (Calm waters), 1906; Hrannir (Waves), 1913;
Vogar (Billows), 1921; and a translation of Henrik Ibsen's Peer
Gynt, first published in 1901 and again in 1922.

NORÐURLJÓS

Eftir Einar Benediktsson

Veit duftsins son nokkra dýrðlegri sýn
en drottnanna hásal í vafurloga?
Sjá grund og vog undir gullhvelfdum boga! —
Hver getur nú unað við spil og vín?
Sjálf moldin er hrein eins og mær við lín;
mókar í haustsins visnu rósum.
Hvert sandkorn í loftsins litum skín
og lækirnir kyssast í silfurrósum.
Við útheimsins skaut er allt eldur og skraut
af iðandi norðurljósum.

Frá sjöunda himni að Ránar rönd
stíga röðlarnir dans fyrir opnum tjöldum,
en ljóshafsins öldur með fjúkandi földum,
falla og ólga við skuggaströnd.
Það er eins og leikið sé huldri hönd
hringspil með glitrandi sprotum og baugum. —
Nú mænir allt dauðlegt á lífsins lönd
frá lokuðum brautum, frá myrkum haugum,
og hrímklettar stara við hljóðan mar
til himins með kristallsaugum.

Nú finnst mér það allt svo lítið og lágt,
sem lifað er fyrir og barizt er móti.
Þó kasti þeir grjóti og hati og hóti
við hverja smásál ég er í sátt.
Því bláloftið hvelfist svo bjart og hátt.
Nú brosir hver stjarna þótt vonirnar svíki,
og hugurinn lyftist í æðri átt.
Nú andar guðs kraftur í duftsins líki.
Vér skynjum vorn þrótt, vér þekkjum í nótt
vorn þegnrétt í ljóssins ríki. —

NORTHERN LIGHTS

Translated by Jakobina Johnson

Was ever such vision to mortals sent
As Northern Lights in the heavens flaming?
The shoreline a golden archway framing.
— Who now is at drinking and cards content? —
The earth lies serene and on sleep intent
Under a cover of roses decaying.
Rare colors the grains of sand present.
— Where waters meet, there is a silver spraying.
The north is aglow with an ornate show,
Of Borealis' displaying.

From the seventh heav'n to the ocean's rim,
The suns hold a dance with the curtain lifted.
And white-capped billows of light are shifted,
— Then break on a strand of shadows dim.
An unseen hand directs at its whim
This glittering round of streamers flowing.
To regions of light from the darkness grim,
All earth-life now turns with fervor growing.
— And a crystal gaze on the glowing haze
The hoary cliffs bestowing.

How base seem the issues — and trifling the call,
That claims our life — or we strive denying.
— Let mortals attack me with hatred defying, —
I now feel at peace with each creature small.
So fair and immense is this vault over all —
And smiling the stars — though our hopes be arrested.
The mind goes soaring, — no heights appal, —
Divine is the power through the dust manifested.
We fathom our strength — our rights are at length
In the kingdom of light attested.

Hve voldugt og djúpt er himinsins haf
og hásigldar snekkjur sem leiðina þreyta.
Að höfninni leita þær, hvort sem þær beita
í horfið — eða þær beygja af.
En aldrei sá neinn þann sem augað gaf
— og uppsprettur ljóssins ei fundnar né skýrðar,
með beygðum knjám og með bænastaf
menn bíða við musteri allrar dýrðar.
En autt er allt sviðið og harðlæst hvert hlið
og hljóður sá andi sem býr þar.

BRIM

Eftir Einar Benediktsson

Volduga hjartaslag hafdjúpsins kalda,
af hljóm þínum drekk ég mér kraft og frið.
Ég heyri í þér skammlífa, skjálfandi alda
skóhljóð tímans, sem fram skal halda,
og blóð mitt þýtur með brimsins nið.

Ég beini sál minni að helsins hafi,
sem handan við sól drekkur lífs míns straum.
Ég sé minn himin með sólbjarmatrafi
við sjóndeild blandast skugganna kafi
og sekk mér í hugar míns dýpsta draum.

Ég sekk mér í brimhljóðsins sogandi öldu
og sál mína að óminnisdjúpinu kný.
Ég tel mig í ætt við unnina köldu,
sem einn af dropunum mældu og töldu,
sem hljómbrot í eilífðarhafsins gný.

How mighty an ocean the heavens bright —
And brave the vessels attempting the sailing.
A haven they seek, with courage unfailing,
Whether they swerve, or their course holds right;
But none have beheld Him who gave us sight,
Nor shown us the source of these marvels abiding.
At the door of His temple, this glorious night,
In homage they pray from their hearts confiding.
— But vainly they wait — for locked is each gate,
And silent the spirit presiding.

SURF

Translated by Skuli Johnson

Thou heart-beat so strong of the sea-depths all cold!
From thy sound for me power and peace new I drain;
I hear in thy short-lived waves veeringly rolled
The footfall of Time that e'er onward must hold
And my blood surges on with the bruit of the main.

My soul I direct down to Death's ocean dim
That beyond the Sun's realm will engulf my life's
                                    stream;
I see that my heavens with sun-brightened brim
Are blent with the shades at the sight's utmost rim
And I sink me down into my mind's deepest dream.

I sink me down into the drawing waves' den
And my soul to the Sea of Oblivion I urge;
I count me in race to the chill waves akin —
A drop the world-waters well-reckoned within,
Or a sound-fragment 'mid the Eternal Sea's surge.

ÞORSTEINN GÍSLASON
(b. 1867)

Þorsteinn Vilhjálmur Gíslason was born at Stærri-Árskógur in the North of Iceland. He was graduated from the College of Iceland in 1892. From 1893 to 1896 he studied Scandinavian philology and literature at the University of Copenhagen. He then returned to Iceland, and has been engaged in journalism — the editor of various papers, including the weekly L ö g - r j e t t a, which he has edited since 1906. Gíslason is an essayist and a translator as well as a journalist and a lyric poet. Among his translations the following may be mentioned: Björnstjerne Björnson's A r n e, Walter Scott's I v a n h o e, and Henryk Sienkiewicz' Q u o V a d i s? Gíslason's first book of poems, K v æ ð i, appeared in 1893; another volume, N o k k u r k v æ ð i (A few poems), appeared in 1904; and a collected edition, L j ó ð m æ l i, was published in 1920.

VORDÆGUR

Eftir Þorstein Gíslason

Ljósið loftin fyllir
og loftin verða blá.
Vorið tánum tyllir
tindana á.

Dagarnir lengjast
og dimman flýr í sjó;
bráðum syngur lóa
í brekku og mó.

ÞORVALDUR THORODDSEN

Eftir Þorstein Gíslason

Yfir eldhraun,
eyðisanda
og sprungna jökla
spor hans liggja.
Fræðasjóði,
sem fólgnir voru,
sótti' hann á öræfi
ættlands síns.

Var hann ungur,
er hann veg sér kaus
um óruddar leiðir
ofar byggðum;
og tröllgeymd
um tugi alda
réð dulskráð
rúnaspjöld.

SPRING

Translated by Skuli Johnson

The air is filled with sunlight,
With azure hue it glows:
The Springtide fair the fell-tops
Touches with her toes.

The day is drawn out longer,
Deep ocean night immures:
Sandpipers soon will sing on
The hillsides and the moors.

THORVALDUR THORODDSEN

Translated by Jakobina Johnson

Over lava-beds,
Sandy barrens
And glaciers vast
The trail has led him.
Hidden treasures
Of precious knowledge
Sought in the wastes
Of his native land.

Young was he
When the way he chose
Which none had known
And none had travelled;
There read the hidden
And mystic runes,
Kept by the trolls
Through countless ages.

Þar af jötnum
jökulhalla
og hulduþjóð
heiðatinda
og eldvættum
undirheima
fræddist hann um fortíð
og framtíð lands.

Gáð var af tindi
glöggu auga
yfir foldu
sem opna bók:
Ýmist jökla
eða elda fingrum
letruð var í berg
landsins saga.

Enginn hefur
eins og hann
lesið leyndarmál
lands og þjóðar.
Enginn sem hann
hefur eyra lagt
við hjartslætti
Heklu foldar.

Enginn hefur rakið
eins og hann
hugsana þræði
horfins tíma.

There from giants
In giant halls
And fairy folk
In peaks and passes,
And the guardians
Of hidden fires,
Learned of his country's
past and present.

From the mountain-peaks
His eagle eye
Scanned his country's
Open pages.
— Either glacial
Or fiery fingers
Inscribed on rocks
A wondrous story.

None before him
Read so wisely
The secret lore
Of land and people.
No one thus
Intently hearkened
To the beating heart
Of Hecla's country.

None before him
So construed
The trend in thought
Of times departed.

Engum manni
eins og honum
legið hefur opin
landsins sál.

Því að huldumál
héraðsvætta
og ljóðskraf
lindadísa
og dvergmál
dökkbjarga
lært hefur hann
og í letur fært.

— — — — —

Sál vors lands
og sagnaheimur
er að hálfu
á heiðum uppi;
en í sveitum
og útverum
og á hafmiðum
að hálfu leyti.

— — — — —

Standa eftir hann
stórvirki
þörf, unnin
þjóð og landi.
Því mun uppi
Þorvalds nafn
meðan Fróns
er í fræðum getið.

And to no one
Had his country
Thus laid bare
Its inmost soul.

For the unknown tongue
Of unseen patrons
And the fairy-tongue
Of founts and rivers
And the dwarf-tongue
In dark cliffs spoken —
— All these he learned
And aptly wrote.

— — — — —

In the valleys
Along our coast-line
Lies merely half
Our world of story.
The other half
Is seen only
From the airy haunts
Of hawk and eagle.

— — — — —

Hence his full
And first-hand knowledge
And the wise thoughts
Of his writings.
While his native land
Is known in story
Shall his honoured name
And works endure.

GUÐMUNDUR FRIÐJÓNSSON
(b. 1869)

Guðmundur Friðjónsson was born at Sílalækur in the North of Iceland. He was graduated from the High School at Möðruvellir in 1893|; he is therefore largely a self-educated man. All his life he has been a farmer. Despite adverse circumstances he has won for himself a prominent place among present-day writers in Iceland. He has been extremely productive. Besides his lyric poetry he has written a great number of short stories, essays, and newspaper articles. As a writer of short stories he ranks very high. A collection of his poems, Úr heima-högum (From the Native Haunts), appeared in 1902; another volume, Kvæði, was published in 1925; and a third volume, Kveðlingar, in 1929.

FEÐGARNIR

Eftir Guðmund Friðjónsson

Hver vinnur eins ágæta vegabót,
þótt verkatíminn sé naumur,
og léttir eins stirðan og fúinn fót
sem feðgarnir: Svefn og draumur?
Þeir leggja eimbrautir austur að sól,
um Atlantshaf þvert og norður á pól,
á sál mína flugham þeir festa,
hinn fegursta, nýjasta og bezta.

Þeir eiga vörubúr fögur og fé,
sem fáum er kunnugt sem skyldi,
þó lána þeir öllum og láta í té,
sem leita á náð þeirra og mildi.
Þar tek ég út allt það sem óskar mín fýst,
sem auga fær séð og tunga lýst.
Til endurgjalds aldrei þó kemur,
en úttektin miljónum nemur.

Mig fýsir að sjá hina fjarlægu storð,
en farkostinn hefi ég eigi.
Og tunguna skortir hin algengu orð
og útsýni, leiðir og vegi.
Á ströndinni sit ég og stari á mar,
er stikar sæinn hið eimknúða far;
og klökkur úr kreppunni rýni
að kvöldroðans purpuralíni.

FATHER AND SON

Translated by Skuli Johnson

Who renders as excellent road-mending though
A workingtime briefer have none,
And lightens the way for feet stiffened and slow
Like Sleep and Dream — father and son?
The routes that they fashion reach east to the sun,
Across the sea west, to the pole north they run,
And they make my soul pinions whereon I am
whirled,
The fairest and newest and best in the world.

They warehouses own and fair wealth too withal
That few know as well as they ought
For freely they lend out on credit to all
Who unto their bounty have sought.
I borrow thence all that I wish for alway —
All eye can behold and all tongue can convey —
And I'm never expected to square the account —
My debts to the pair now to millions amount.

I'm eager to visit a far distant land
But dearth of ships faring delays
I lack too the words that success can command,
The vision, the routes and the ways.
On shore hence I sit and I out to sea stare
And see their great steamer o'er Ocean's ways fare,
From my straits here I gaze till with heart touched
I view
The hangings of evening purple in hue.

Hvort jörðin er gráofnum grímuhjúp sveipt,
eða glitskikkju vorsólar búin,
er gulltoppu feðganna á himininn hleypt,
af himnesku eldfjöri knúin.
Þeir eiga verksmiðju austur frá sól.
á aljarðarstraumum og norður á pól.
Úr geislunum glitvef þeir búa
og glerþráð úr krystöllum snúa.

Í himininn flytja þeir fýst mína í sel,
er flýja mig vökunnar annir;
þá renni ég göndum um ragnahvel
og reikistjarnanna hrannir.
Því draumvonin býr fyrir handan höf
á hæðinni sunnan og ofan við gröf,
í al-laufgum, angandi runni
hjá ódáins ljósveiga brunni.

HVAÐ VANTAR ÍSLENZKU ÞJÓÐINA MEST?

Eftir Guðmund Friðjónsson

Eld árvakran
á arni, er vermi
hugskot heimamanns;
eld, sem áhuga
yfirvalda
geti úr dróma drepið.

And whether the Earth assumes autumn's cowl grey
Or springtide's cloak bright-hued she wears,
The twain on steed Gilt-Tuft mount Heaven's
                                        steep way —
With vigour divine urged, he fares.
A factory have they too east of the Dawn —
It reaches the pole and rests world-streams upon —
And they weave webs of light their great workshop
                                                within,
And gossamer-threads out af crystal they spin.

To heaven they bring me a while to abide
When Waking's cares from me have fled;
I then, on a magic mount, Heaven's vault ride,
Mid myriad starry hosts sped;
For hopes wherewith Sleep and his Son, Dream,
                                        us dower
Dwell far beyond seas, in a fragrant green bower,
To the south of the grave, on a sun-smitten height
Beside the eternal world's well-spring of light.

"WHAT LACK WE?"
(Abridged)
(The question was put by an Icelandic periodical)
Translated by Jakobina Johnson

An early fire
And ever-burning
On the hearth of home.
— A rousing fire
That ruling minds
May shed the withes of sleep.

Trú, sem fjöll flytji
og farartálma
Þránd úr þjóðgötu;
trú, er sólseturs
silfurnámu
metur sem morgungull.

Brestur barnstygi
og brúðkaupsföt
alþjóðar innri mann;
lýtur ljósþrá
í lægra haldi
fyrir hyggju heims.

Út á æfimar
einstaklinga
vantar stjörnu í stafn.
Skortir skutbúa,
er skerst í odda,
úrvals áttavita.

— — — —

Leggur á lífsgleði
læðing sterkan,
Gleipni grárra magna,
kýldur konungur
kaldrifjaður
— hylltur aldarandi.

— — — —

Brestur borgara,
bændur, forkólfa,
lífsins lýsigull —
eldmóð eilífrar
íturhyggju
konungs, er krossinn bar.

Faith to move mountains,
And all obstructions
From the road of progress;
And welcome the silver
Found at sundown,
As well as the morning's gold.

Our spirit knows not
Youthful ways,
Nor festive bridal raiment.
Desire for light
Is dominated
By worldly needs and cares.

On our voyage
Every helms-man
Needs a guiding star;
And the mariners
— Oft divided —
Need a compass true.
— — — —
Our joy of life
Lacks free expression, —
Fettered by forces dark
Led by a proud king
And cold-hearted:
The vogue of any age.
— — — —
All our leaders —
And rank and file,
Lack the flaming torch
Of a direct
And daring purpose
Held by the king of the Cross.

Vantar á varðberg
vökufúsan
vafurloga vita,
þann er þjóð vorri,
er þrautir vaxa,
gerist glóðafeykir

Einstigs áfanga
upp í móti
gengur gæfa skyggn;
á þeim upplöndum
aftanroði
fagnar afturelding.

Á því upplendi
auga lítur
útsæ endalausan —
haf, sem hefur
í hulinsfaðmi
perlu-móður-mið.

Gefi guðs mildi
geisla, er lýsi
einstigi og almanna leið,
hlýju í hugskot,
himin alstirndan,
borg, sem engi brýtur.

Beacons we lack,
Ever watchful —
And ever burning bright,
From which the nation
May derive
Courage in times of peril.

— — — — —

Leads a lone path
To levels high
Affording spacious vision;
Seen from those uplands
The even-glow
Lingers till dawn of day.

From those uplands
The eye may see
A boundless, sweeping ocean.
— An ocean holding
In its bosom
Precious mother-of-pearl.

May kindly rays
From heaven illumine
Lonely path and highway.
And minds responsive
Find the starry dome
A mighty source of strength.

GUÐMUNDUR MAGNÚSSON
1873—1918

Guðmundur Magnússon was born at Rif, "the northernmost farm in Iceland". He was brought up in poverty and thus deprived of all educational advantages in youth. For years he was a farm hand and a fisherman. In 1893 he became a printer's apprentice, first in Seyðisfjörður and later in Reykjavík; he worked as a printer in Copenhagen from 1896 to 1898, reading and studying on the side. From then until his death he resided in Reykjavík, earning his livelihood as a printer, but devoting all his spare time to writing. In 1903 a grant from the Icelandic government enabled him to travel extensively in England and on the continent. From 1910 on he received an annual stipend from the government in recognition of his literary work. Magnússon — he wrote most of his works under the pseudonym J ó n T r a u s t i — was primarily a novelist and a writer of short stories, one of the foremost among his contemporaries. He also wrote essays and lyric poetry. Three volumes of his poems have appeared: H e i m a o g e r l e n d i s (At home and abroad), 1899; Í s l a n d s v í s u r (Iceland-lays), 1903; and K v æ ð a b ó k, a collected edition, in 1922.

DRAUMALANDIÐ

Eftir Guðmund Magnússon

Ó, leyf mér þig að leiða
til landsins fjalla heiða
   með sælu sumrin löng.
Þar angar blóma breiða
við blíðan fuglasöng.

Þar aðeins yndi fann ég,
þar aðeins við mig kann ég,
   þar batt mig tryggða band,
því þar er allt sem ann ég. —
Það er mitt draumaland.

RÓÐUR

Eftir Guðmund Magnússon

Bráðum birtir af degi,
belta sig skýin létt.
Tunglið er hátt yfir heiðum,
hafið blikandi slétt.
Leika í löngum glömpum
líðandi öldubök.
Heyrast heiman frá vörum
Hraustmannleg áratök.

MY LAND OF DREAMS

Translated by Paul Bjarnason

O, come with me to my land,
With moor and heathered highland
    And summers sweet and long —
A beauteous inland island
    Alive with scent and song.

No other place appeased me,
Each pretty charm that seized me
    With tender mem'ries teems,
It's all that ever pleased me.
    It is my land of dreams.

OARAGE

Translated by Skuli Johnson

The night draws nigh to the dawning,
The clouds don belt-streaks of light,
The moon hangs high o'er the heathlands,
The sea is splendidly bright;
Ripples with glitter far-gleaming
Upon the waters appear:
Mariners strike out from haven —
Their sturdy oarage we hear.

GUÐMUNDUR GUÐMUNDSSON
(1874—1919)

Guðmundur Guðmundsson was born at Hrólfsstaðahellir in the South of Iceland. He was graduated from the College of Iceland in 1897. For some time he studied medicine. From 1906 to 1909 he was engaged in journalistic work at Ísafjörður, but the greater part of his life he devoted to writing. He was first and last a lyric poet, but he also wrote many articles for papers and periodicals. He published the following volumes of poems: Ljóðmæli, 1900; Strengleikar (Lays), 1903; Gígjan (The Fiddle), 1906; Friður á jörðu (Peace on Earth), 1911, second edition 1913; Ljósaskifti (Twilight), 1913; and Ljóð og kvæði (Songs and Poems), 1917. Guðmundsson translated many poems into Icelandic, including Tennyson's Locksley Hall. A volume of his translations, Erlend ljóð, was published in 1924.

FORMÁLI AÐ „FRIÐ Á JÖRÐU"

Eftir Guðmund Guðmundsson

Friðarins guð, in hæsta hugsjón mín,
höndunum lyfti ég í bæn til þín!
Kraftarins faðir, kraftaverkið gjörðu:
Gefðu mér dýrðar þinnar sólarsýn,
sigrandi mætti gæddu ljóðin mín, —
sendu mér kraft að syngja frið á jörðu.

Kærleikans guð, af sál mér sviptu hjúp,
sjón minni birtu lífsins eymdadjúp,
þaðan, sem andvörp þúsundanna stíga!
Sjá, fætur þína tárin titra við,
tindrandi augun mæna, og biðja um frið, —
friðarins dögg á hrjóstrin láttu hníga!

Spekinnar guð, lát spádómskraftinn þinn
spakmálum þínum göfga anda minn,
birtu mér lágum það sem hylst þeim háu:
kærleikans undra-mátt, — við hljóm og hreim
hörpunnar minnar, láttu af krafti þeim
huggast og gleðjast hina smáðu' og smáu!

Friðarins guð, ég finn þitt hjarta slá
föðurmilt, blítt og sterkt í minni þrá,
brennandi þrá, að mýkja meinin hörðu.
Því finn ég mínum vængjum vaxa flug,
viljanum traust og strengjum mínum dug
til þess að syngja, — syngja frið á jörðu.

"PEACE ON EARTH" (PROLOGUE)

Translated by Jakobina Johnson

Lord, God of peace, my spirit's high ideal,
To Thee I lift my hands in mute appeal,
Omnipotent, a miracle imploring.
Grant to my soul a vision of Thy light,
Charge Thou my song with Thy compelling might,
That it may rise — Thy peace on earth restoring.

Lord, God of love, unto my spirit show
In all their truth the depths of human woe,
Where-from the groans of multitudes are calling.
Mingled with tears they rise around Thy feet,
Beseeching looks of dying eyes entreat:
'Thy peace on earth, like dew on deserts falling'.

Lord, God of wisdom, with prophetic fires
Cleanse Thou my soul, ennoble my desires,
Thy purpose to my lowly heart revealing.
Thy wonder-power of love in song and sound
Call from my harp in rhapsody profound,
The suffering and broken spirits healing.

Lord, God of peace, Thy beating heart impels
Mine own, when that with sweet compassion swells,
Thy mercy for the sufferers imploring.
Wherefore I feel my spirit's wings grow strong
And courage rise to wake my harp in song.
O, may it rise — Thy peace on earth restoring.

JÓHANN SIGURJÓNSSON
(1880—1919)

Jóhann Sigurjónsson was born at Laxamýri in the North of
Iceland. He was a student in the College of Iceland from 1896
to 1899. For some time he studied veterinary surgery at the
Royal Veterinary School in Copenhagen; but he soon became
interested in literary work and devoted his whole time to it.
He lived in Copenhagen and wrote mostly in Danish. He
holds a high place among present-day Scandinavian dramatists.
His best known drama, Fjalla-Eyvindur (Eyvind of the
Hills), has been presented in all the Scandinavian countries as
well as in Germany and in America. (For English translation,
see Scandinavian Classics, Vol. vi). Sigurjónsson's
lyric poems have appeared in Icelandic periodicals. A small
volume of his poems in Danish, Smaadigte (Verses), appeared in 1920.

SONNETTA
Eftir Jóhann Sigurjónsson

Vorið er liðið, ilmur ungra daga
orðinn að þungum, sterkum sumarhita,
æskan er horfin, engir draumar lita
ókomna tímans gráa sinuhaga.

Við erum fæddir úti á eyðiskaga,
eilífðarsjórinn hefur dimma vita,
fánýtar skeljar fyrir blóð og svita
fengum við keyptar, það er mannsins saga.

Þó hef ég aldrei elskað daginn heitar
— eilífðar nafnið stafar barnsins tunga —
fátæka líf, að þínum knjám ég krýp,
áþekkur skuggablómi, er ljóssins leitar,
— leggurinn veldur naumast eigin þunga —
fórnandi höndum þína geisla ég gríp.

SORG
Eftir Jóhann Sigurjónsson

Vei, vei, yfir hinni föllnu borg!
Hvar eru þín stræti,
þínir turnar,
og ljóshafið, yndi næturinnar?
Eins og kórall í djúpum sjó
varst þú undir bláum himninum,
eins og sylgja úr drifnu silfri
hvílir þú á brjóstum jarðarinnar.

A SONNET

Translated by Skuli Johnson

Spring has departed; early days' sweet scent
Has changed to summer's sultry pungency;
Our youth has gone, no dream-flecked galaxy
Decks the grey fields of days that are unspent.

We're born upon a headland bare and rent
By the dim-beaconed sea, Eternity!
With sweat and blood — such is man's history! —
We've bought some shells and lo, our lives are spent!

And yet I've ne'er loved more the day's dear sight.
— "Eternity" the lips of infants bear —
Before thee, Life, I bow on bended knees;
E'en as a shaded flow'ret looks for light
— The stalk can scarcely its own weight upbear —
With suppliant hands, thy shining rays I seize.

SORROW

Translated by Magnús Á. Árnason

Woe, woe, unto the fallen city!
Where are thy streets,
Thy towers,
And thy sea of lights, the joy of night?
Like a coral in the bosom of the ocean
Thou dwelt beneath the blue sky.
Like a brooch of purest silver
Thou rested on the breasts of earth.

Vei, vei!
Í dimmum brunnum vaka eitursnákar
og nóttin aumkast yfir þínum rústum.

Jóreykur lífsins þyrlast til himna,
menn í aktygjum,
vitstola konur í gylltum kerrum.
— Gefið mér salt að eta, svo tungan skorpni
í mínum munni
og minn harmur þagni.

Á hvítum hesti hleyptum við upp á bláan him-
            inbogann
og lékum að gylltum knöttum;
við héngum í faxi myrkursins
þegar það steyptist í gegnum undirdjúpin:
eins og tunglsgeislar sváfum við á bylgjum hafsins.

Hvar eru þau fjöll, sem hrynja yfir mína sorg,
hálsar, sem skýla minni nekt með dufti?
Í svartnætti eilífðarinnar flýgur rauður dreki
og spýr eitri.
Sól eftir sól hrynja í dropatali
og fæða nýtt líf og nýja sorg.

Woe, woe!
Down in dark wells poisonous snakes are crawling,
But night takes pity on thy ruins.

The hoofs of life whirl dust into the sky, —
Men in harness,
Insane women in golden chariots.
— Give me salt to eat, that my tongue be parched
within my mouth
And silenced by my sorrow.

On white horses we rode into the blue arch of
heaven
And played with golden spheres;
We hung on to the mane of darkness
While it plunged through the abyss of space;
And we slept like moonbeams on the ocean waves.

Where are the mountains, that shall crumble over
my sorrow,
Hills, that shall hide my nakedness with dust?
A red dragon flies through eternity's darkest night
And spews poison.
Sun after sun fall drop by drop
And bear new life, new sorrow.

UNNUR BENEDIKTSDÓTTIR
(b. 1881)

Unnur Benediktsdóttir was born at Auðnir in the North of
Iceland. She is the wife of S. Sigfússon, the director of the
Farmers' Cooperative Society at Húsavík. She has published
the following collections of lyric poetry: Kvæði, 1909;
Syngi, syngi svanir mínir (Sing, sing, my Swans), 1916;
Segðu mér að sunnan (What News from the South), 1920;
and Við yzta haf (By the outermost Sea). She has also
written a number of short stories. She writes under the
pseudonym Hulda.

EINS OG ÚR BLÓMABIKAR

Eftir Unni Benediktsdóttur

Eins og úr blómabikar
hið bláa daggartár,
svo hurfu harmar mínir
um heiðrík bernskuár.
En nú ei þrá mín þrýtur
í þrungnum hugarreit,
hún er sem byrgður brunnur,
sem birtu aldrei leit

TUNGLSGEISLI

Eftir Unni Benediktsdóttur

Ef að tunglsgeislinn
litli, ljósi,
hefði fjaðrir
og flogið gæti
á vængjum hvítum
yfir vog og strönd,
eg skyldi hann
með ást mína senda.

Ef að tunglsgeislinn
litli, ljósi,
hefði mannamál,
skyldi ég biðja' hann
að bera mína
ungu ástarkveðju.

AS FROM A FLOWER'S CHALICE

Translated by Skuli Johnson

As from a flower's chalice
The dewdrops disappear
So passed my sorrows from me
When days were young and dear.
A yearning now enthralls me
And nowise can be quelled;
'Tis like a secret fountain
The sun has ne'er beheld.

IF THE MOONBEAM

Translated by Skuli Johnson

If the moonbeam,
Airy and bright,
Feathers possessed
And the power of flight:
On his pinions of snow,
I would ask him to go,
O'er ocean and land
At my love's command.

If the moonbeam,
Tiny and bright,
Power possessed
That on words could alight:
On his pinions of snow,
I would ask him to go,
Across the wide air
My love-greetings to bear.

Ef að tunglsgeislinn
ljúfi, ljósi,
hefði vanga og vör,
skyldi ég biðja' hann
í blundi kyssa
hann, er ég heitast ann.

If the moonbeam,
Gentle and bright,
Features possessed
That would charm with their sight:
On his pinions of snow,
I would ask him to go,
And love's kiss impart
To the lad of my heart.

STEFÁN FRÁ HVÍTADAL
(b. 1884)

Stefán Sigurðsson frá Hvítadal was born at Hólmavík in the North of Iceland. He is a self-educated man, and has for years been a farmer. His first volume of poetry, Söngvar förumannsins (The Beggar's Songs), appeared in 1916, a second edition in 1919; this was followed by Óður einyrkjans (The Song of the Solitary Worker), 1921; Heilög kirkja (Holy Church), 1924; and Helsingjar (Geese), 1927.

ÞÉR KONUR

Eftir Stefán frá Hvítadal

Þér konur, með víðfaðma vængi
og vonir, er djarfar blossa,
. . . Þér springið út og ilmið
við ástir, faðmlög og kossa.
    Að lokum fölnar og fellur
    hver fjóla og anganreyr
    . . . en kynslóð af kynslóð fæðist
    og kyssir, starfar og deyr.

Þér konur, mig óskiptan eigið
í æfinnar slysum og láni.
. . . Og yður hyllir mitt hjarta,
þótt hár mitt fölni og gráni.
    Ég breiði fagnandi út faðminn
    — sjá fríður guðs heimur er
    . . . og enn þá er ilmur úr grasi
    og æska í hjarta mér.

Þér konur á eldblysum kveikið,
er kveldsól að viði hnígur,
. . . svo reykelsis ilmur og andakt
frá ölturum mannanna stígur,
    — unz lyfta sér vængjaðar verur
    í vorhvolfin töfrafríð.
    — Og þetta er sannorð saga
    og söm frá ómunatíð.

Þér konur, sem ungir vér unnum,
í Edens sólríka lundi,
. . . þá urðum vér konungar allir,
en almúgagervið hrundi,

YOU WOMEN

Translated by Erl. G. Gillies

You women, with high heart's desires,
And brave hopes, all doubts dismissing,
— You burst into blossom and fragrance,
By loving, embracing and kissing.
  Finally withered and fallen
  The fairest violet lies,
  The present, like past generations,
  Kisses and labors and dies.

To you I belong undivided,
— Whatever betide me may
— My heart will ever hail you,
Though the hair on my head turn gray. —
  I joyfully open my bosom,
  — How fair is God's world in each part!
  — And still the grasses smell sweetly
  And youth is still in my heart.

You women, you light the torches,
When the sun to the sea descends,
And sweet smell of incense, and reverence
From the Altars of men ascends,
  Till bright winged beings are wafted
  Into the fair vernal sky.
  — And this is an ever true story
  Repeated in all times gone by.

You women, who won our first love,
Where youth's Eden's blossoms were spread,
Then mighty kings all became we,
And the plebeian garb was shed.

Vér rísum með yður allir,
sem elskum og verðum til,
... því listinni gefið þér lífið
og lífinu sól og yl.

Þér konur, sem hetjurnar hófuð
mót hækkandi sól og degi,
... Eg þakka yður feðranna framsókn
og framann úr austur vegi.
    Nú ljómar sá orrustu-aðall
    við aldanna sjónarrönd,
    ... þeir konungar elskuðu allir,
    sem unnu borgir og lönd.

Þér leidduð hinn volduga' og vísa
að vizkunnar göfga brunni,
— Þér Zíons- sólbrenndu -dætur,
er Salomó konungur unni.
    Og málminn fylltuð þér mildi
    og musterið reis við yl.
    ... Og því loga Salomós söngvar
    að Súlamít hans var til.

Þér konur, sem hallirnar hækkið
og hefjið mannanna sonu,
... hve Eysteins „Lilja" er innfjálg
af ást hans til jarðneskrar konu.
    Þér hækkið vort andlega heiði,
    unz himnarnir opnir sjást.
    — Hver dáð, sem maðurinn drýgir,
    er draumur um konu ást.

You lift us, who love you, up higher,
Give strength to us in our strife,
To art you bring inspiration,
And warmth and light to our life.

You women, who lifted the heroes
To a light of a brighter day.
For the forefathers' progress and eastern
Culture accept you my thanks, I pray!
  Now blaze those battle-famed heroes
  The far past's horizon above;
  The conquerors of countries and cities
  Were all made greater by love.

You led the wise and the mighty,
Where the fountain of wisdom did flow.
You sunburnt daughters of Zion,
Beloved of King Solomo.
  You mellowness gave to the metal,
  Made the Temple rise fair and complete,
  And Solomo's songs are glowing
  Because of his Sulamith.

You prominence lend to a palace,
Add merit and honour to man.
— — How "Lilja" by Eysteinn, is richer,
Because of his love for a woman.
  You widen the spiritual vision,
  Till open the heavens above;
  And all our noblest achievements
  Are dreams of a woman's love.

DAVÍÐ STEFÁNSSON FRÁ FAGRASKÓGI
(b. 1895)

Davíð Stefánsson was born at Fagraskógur in the North of
Iceland. He was graduated from the College of Iceland in 1919.
He has for some years been a librarian at Akureyri. He is very
productive and has already published the following books of
poems: Svartar fjaðrir (Black Feathers), 1919; Kvæði,
1922; Kveðjur (Greetings), 1924; and Ný kvæði, 1929.
He has also published a drama.

ÁLFAHÓLL

Eftir Davíð Stefánsson

Þó fjúki á fornar slóðir
og fenni í gömul skjól,
geta ekki fönnin og frostið
falið Álfahól.

Yfir hann skeflir aldrei,
þótt allt sé af gaddi hvítt,
því eldur brennur þar inni,
sem ísinn getur þítt.

Þar á ég höfði að halla,
þó hríðin byrgi sól,
fjúki á fornar slóðir
og fenni í gömul skjól

ELDUR Í ÖSKUNNI LEYNIST

Eftir Davíð Stefánsson

Eldur í öskunni leynist
og ást í þögulli sál.
— Bikarnum lyfti ég bleikur
og bergi þína skál.

Við bálið bergðum við áður
úr bikarnum eitrað vín.
Ég lofaði að yrkja aldrei
ástarljóð til þín.

Í dreggjunum drekk ég hljóður
dauðans og þína skál.
— — Eldur i öskunni leynist
og ást í þöglri sál.

"FAIRY HILL"

Translated by Skuli Johnson

Though ice close the ancient pathways
And snows the old shelters fill,
The sleet and the snow-fall can never
Envelop Fairy Hill.

Above it drifts never gather
Though frost-bound the whole land lies,
For within it blazes forever
A fire that melts the ice.

Here have I a haven of refuge
From lowering storm-clouds ill,
Though ice close the ancient pathways
And snows the old shelters fill.

OFT FLAMES AMID ASHES LIE HIDDEN

Translated by Skuli Johnson

Oft flames amid ashes lie hidden
And love in a reticent soul,
Lo, pallid I lift up the chalice
and drain in thine honour the bowl.

Aforetime we drank by the fire
A beaker of venom-mixed wine;
I vowed then that love of thee never
Would merge with the lays that are mine.

To Death and to thee now in silence
I drain the last lees of the bowl.
Oft flames amid ashes lie hidden
And love in a reticent soul.

BRÚÐARSKÓRNIR

Eftir Davíð Stefánsson

Alein sat hún við öskustóna,.
— Hugurinn var fram á Melum.
Hún var að brydda sér brúðarskóna,
— Sumir gera allt í felum.

Úr augum hennar skein ást og friður.
— Hver verður húsfreyja á Melum?
Hún lauk við skóna og læsti þá niður.
— Sumir gera allt í felum.

. . . Alein grét hún við öskustóna.
Gott á húsfreyjan á Melum.
Í eldinum brenndi hún brúðarskóna.
— Sumir gera allt í felum.

SKUGGINN

Eftir Davíð Stefánsson

Sem hjarta Guðs
er ég hreinn í kvöld,
fagur sem óskir hans
og frjáls sem hans völd.

Alla vil ég gleðja.
Fyrir alla þjást.
— — Í kvöld er ég skuggi
af konu ást.

THE BRIDE'S SLIPPERS

Translated by Skuli Johnson

Alone she sate by the hearth-place biding.
— Her mind lingered far off out at Dune —
She was abroidering bridal-shoon.
Some do everything in hiding.

Her eyes beamed calmness and love confiding.
— And who will be house-wife out at Dune? —
She finished and shut away the shoon.
Some do everything in hiding.

Alone, she wept by the hearth-place biding.
— How blest is the house-wife out at Dune! —
She brought out and burnt the bridal-shoon.
Some do everything in hiding.

THE SHADOW

Translated by Skuli Johnson

Like God's own heart
I'm pure tonight,
Fair as His wishes all
And free as His might.

All men would I gladden,
For all would I smart:
I'm the shade of the love in
A woman's heart.

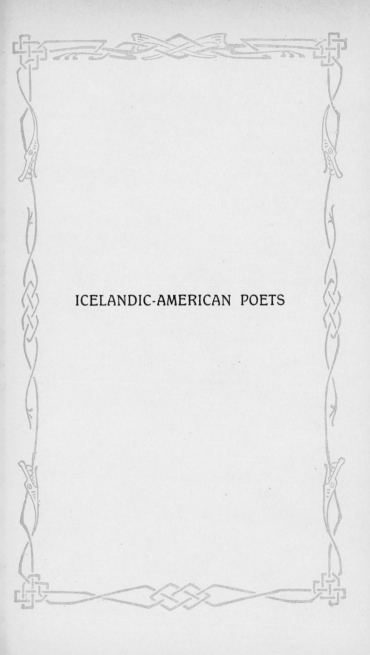

ICELANDIC-AMERICAN POETS

STEPHAN G. STEPHANSSON

(1853—1927)

Stephan Guðmundsson Stephansson was born at Kirkjuhóll in the North of Iceland. He was the son of a farmer. With his parents he emigrated to America in 1873. He was three times a pioneer, first in Wisconsin in 1874; then in North Dakota in 1880; and lastly in Markerville, Alberta, in 1889. Here he lived as a farmer until his death. He never attended any school, but was an unusually widely read man, as his poems best reveal. Despite the hard toil of pioneer farm-life, Stephansson was a very prolific writer. And he has an undisputed place among the greatest of Icelandic poets. His first book of poems, Úti á víðavangi (In the Open Air) appeared in 1894; this was followed by Á ferð og flugi (Faring and Flying), 1900; a collected edition, Andvökur (Wakeful Nights), Vol. I—III, 1909—1910; Heimleiðis (Homewards), 1917; Vígslóði (The Wartrail), 1920; and Andvökur, Vol. IV—V, 1923.

ÞÓTT ÞÚ LANGFÖRULL LEGÐIR

Eftir Stephan G. Stephansson

Þótt þú langförull legðir
sérhvert land undir fót,
bera hugur og hjarta
samt þíns heimalandsmót,
frænka eldfjalls og íshafs,
sifji árfoss og hvers,
dóttir langholts og lyngmós,
sonur landvers og skers!

Yfir heim eða himin,
hvert sem hugar þín önd,
skreyta fossar og fjallshlíð
öll þín framtíðarlönd!
Fjarst í eilífðar útsæ
vakir eylendan þín.
Nóttlaus voraldar veröld,
þar sem víðsýnið skín.

Það er óskaland íslenzkt,
sem að yfir þú býr,
aðeins blómgróin björgin,
sérhver baldjökull hlýr.
Frænka eldfjalls og íshafs,
sifji árfoss og hvers,
dóttir langholts og lyngmós,
sonur landvers og skers!

FROM AN ADDRESS AT AN ICELANDIC CELEBRATION

Translated by Skuli Johnson

Though all lands in long travels
You should lay 'neath your feet —
In your mind and your heart yet
Your old homeland's marks meet!
You volcano and ice-sea
Fall and geyser-fount bore!
Bred nigh scree-height and ling-heath!
Heir to skerry and shore!

O'er all earth and the heavens
In your thoughts you may fare,
Still your falls and your fell-slopes
All your Future's lands bear!
Near Eternity's sea-rim
Your dear isle doth abide
Like world of Spring nightless
Where the outlook is wide.

'Tis mid dream-haunts Icelandic
That your heart-hopes e'er dwell;
Wherein thawed is each glacier
And enflowered each fell!
You, volcano and ice-sea
Fall and geyser-fount bore!
Bred nigh scree-height and ling-heath!
Heir to skerry and shore!

VIÐ VERKALOK

Eftir Stephan G. Stephansson

Er sólskins hlíðar sveipast aftanskugga
  um sumarkvöld,
og máninn hengir hátt í greinar trjánna
  sinn hálfa skjöld.
Er kveldkul andsvalt aftur kæla tekur
  mitt enni sveitt,
og eftir dagsverk friðnum nætur fagnar
  hvert fjörmagn þreytt.

Er út' á grundum hringja bjöllur hjarða
  nú hljótt, svo glöggt,
og kveld-ljóð fugls í skógnum einstakt ómar
  og angur-klökkt,
og golan virðist tæpa á hálfri hending
  er hæst 'ún hvín,
og hlátur barna, er leika sér við lækinn,
  berst ljúft til mín.

En eins og tunglskins blettir akrar blika
  við blárri grund,
og ljósgrá móða leitin bakkafyllir
  og lægð og sund,
og neðst í austri gylltar stjörnur glitra
  í gegnum skóg:
Þá sit ég úti undir húsa-gafli
  í aftan-ró.

Því hjarta mitt er fullt af hvíld og fögnuð',
  af frið' mín sál.
þá finnst mér aðeins yndi, blíða, fegurð
  sé alheims mál.

AT CLOSE OF DAY

Translated by Jakobina Johnson

When sunny hills are draped in velvet shadows,
    By Summer Night —
And Lady Moon hangs out among the tree tops
    Her crescent bright;
And when the welcome evening breeze is cooling
    My fevered brow —
And all who toil, rejoice that blessed night time
    Approaches now; —

When out among the herds the bells are tingling,
    Now clear, now faint —
And in the woods a lonely bird is voicing
    His evening plaint;
And when the breeze with drowsy accent whispers
    Its melody —
And from the brook the joyous cries of children
    Are borne to me; —

When fields of grain have caught a gleam of moonlight,
    But dark the ground; —
A pearl-gray mist has filled to over-flowing
    The dells around;
Some golden stars are peeping forth to brighten
    The eastern wood; —
Then I am resting out upon my doorstep,
    In nature's mood.

My heart reflects the rest and sweet rejoicing
    Around, above;
And beauty is the universal language
    And peace and love;

Að allir hlutir biðji bænum mínum
　　og blessi mig.
Við nætur gæzku-hjartað jörð og himinn
　　að hvíli sig.

En þegar hinzt er allur dagur úti
　　og uppgerð skil,
og hvað sem kaupið veröld kann að virða
　　sem vann ég til:
í slíkri ró ég kysi mér að kveða
　　eins klökkvan brag,
og rétta heimi að síðstu sáttar-hendi
　　um sólarlag.

KVÖLD

Eftir Stephan G. Stephansson

Í rökkrinu, þegar ég orðinn er einn
og af mér hef reiðingnum velt,
og jörðin vor hefur sjálfa sig
frá sól inn í skuggann elt,
og mælginni sjálfri sígur í brjóst
og sofnar við hundanna gelt.

En lífsönnin dottandi í dyrnar er sezt,
sem daglengis vörður minn er,
sem styggði upp léttfleygu ljóðin mín öll
svo liðu þau sönglaust frá mér,
sem vængbraut þá hugsun, sem hóf sig á loft
og himininn ætlaði sér.

And all things seem to join in benediction
    And prayers for me;
And at Night's loving heart, both earth and heaven
    At rest I see.

And when the last of all my days is over: —
    The last page turned;
And what-so-ever shall be deemed in wages
    That I have earned: —
In such a mood I hope to be composing
    My sweetest lay;
And then, — extend my hand to all the world
    And pass away.

EVENING

Translated by Jakobina Johnson

At twilight, when I am alone with my thoughts,
— The trappings of labour have shed, —
Our earth, in pursuit of its ceaseless round,
From light into shadow fled —
And garrulous talk to its ultimate end
The baying of hounds has sped,

And Care on my doorstep sits drowsy at last,
— Who guards all my movements by day,
Who startled my songs — all the lightest of wing —
And silent they fluttered away,
Who bruised the wing of a thought as it soared
Its heavenward call to obey.

Hve sárfeginn gleymdi ég og sættist við allt,
ef sjálfráður mætti ég þá
í kyrrðinni og dimmunni dreyma það land
sem dagsljósið skein ekki á,
þar æ upp af skipsreika skolast hún von
og skáldanna reikula þrá.

Það landið, sem ekki með o'nálag hátt
í upphæðum neitt getur bætzt,
þar einkis manns velferð er volæði hins,
né valdið er takmarkið hæst,
og sigurinn aldrei er sársauki neins,
en sanngirni er boðorðið æðst.

En þá birtist andvakan ferleg og föl
og fælir burt hvíld mína og ró,
og glötuðu sálirnar sækja að mér,
sem sviku það gott í þeim bjó,
og útburðir mannlífsins ýlfra þá hátt —
það atgervi er hirðulaust dó.

Og þá sé ég opnast það eymdanna djúp,
þar erfiðið liggur á knjám,
en iðjulaust fjársafn af féleysi elst
sem fúinn í lifandi trjám,
en hugstola mannfjöldans vitund og vild
er villt um og stjórnað af fám.

Þar jafnan eins vafasöm viðskipti öll
og vinar-þel mannanna er
sem einliðans, dagaða uppi um kvöld
hjá útlögztum ræningja her,
sem hlustar með lokuðum augunum á,
að óvinir læðast að sér.

— How fain to forgive and forget would I rest
If I, my own master once more,
Through soft-falling darkness and silence could dream
The sweet but invisible shore
That claims all our hopes which are shipwrecked in life,
And longings, which poets adore.

Where wealth that is gathered by taxes or tolls
Or tariffs — is counted as vain.
Where no man's success is another man's loss,
Nor power the goal and the gain,
— The first of commandments is justice to all,
And victory causes no pain.

Then looms up before me, all ghastly and pale,
A night-time of sleepless unrest.
And I am surrounded by spectres of souls
Who failed to live up to their best.
And hark to the cry of the foundlings of life:
— Abilities shunned and represt.

And then I see men in a woeful abyss
Whom toil has forced to their knees,
But indolent Greed on their helplessness thrives,
— Disease at the heart of our trees, —
And masses bereft of their reason and will
Are baited and governed by these, —

With dealings and friendships as doubtful as those
Awaiting the wanderer slow
Whom night overtakes as he sees in dismay
A bandits' encampment below, —
— And hears through the darkness, while feigning
                                        to sleep,
The stealthy approach of the foe.

Og villu-nótt mannkyns um veglausa jörð
svo voða-löng orðin mér finnst,
sem framfara skíman sé skröksaga ein,
og skuggarnir enn hafi ei þynnzt.
Því jafnvel í fornöld sveif hugur eins hátt —
og hvar er þá nokkuð sem vinnst?

Jú, þannig, að menningin út á við eykst
hver öld þó að beri hana skammt —
hún dýpkar ei, hækkar ei, lengir þó leið
sem langdegis sólskinið jafnt.
En augnabliks vísirinn, æfin manns stutt,
veit ekkert um muninn þann samt.

En jafnvel í smalanna einveru inn,
sem árgeislinn, læðist hún rótt
og bjarmar í hugum þó beri ei á,
því birtingin fer þar svo hljótt —
og ég, sem get kveðið við kolsvartan heim
slíkt kvæði um andvöku-nótt.

Og hugar-rór stigið í hvíluna þá
að hinztu, sem við ég ei skil:
Svo viss, að í heiminum vari þó enn
hver von mín með ljós sitt og yl,
það lifi, sem bezt var í sálu mín sjálfs —
að sólskinið verður þó til!

— The night of our wand'rings seems woefully long,
The wayfarers lost as of yore,
Our dawn of advancement a boastful romance,
The shadows as dense as before.
The minds of the ancients soared equally high,
Where, then, is our wonderful score?

In this — that the dawn reaches numbers increased
Through centuries slipping away.
— Not higher — nor deeper — but Farther it seeks
Like shafts of the lengthening day.
On brief wingéd moments each lifetime departs,
And sees but the tragic delay.

For even the shepherds on moorlands afar
Have felt this benevolent ray
Of slow-creeping dawn, as it touches their hearts,
Transforming their arduous day —
And mine — this unquenchable longing to sing
Which sleepless at night I obey,

Till finally called — and shall calmly retire
Where sleeplessness may not assail,
Assured that whatever of good I conceived
Continues — and never shall fail.
The best that was in me for ever shall live,
The sun over darkness prevail.

KRISTINN STEFÁNSSON
(1856—1916)

Kristinn Stefánsson was born at Egilsá in the North of Iceland. He emigrated to America 1873; for some years he lived in Ontario, but from 1881 until his death he made his home in Winnipeg. Stefánsson was an entirely self-taught man, widely read in English, American, and Scandinavian literature. A small volume of his poems, Vestan hafs (West of the Ocean) appeared in 1900; a collected edition, Út um vötn og velli (Midst Lakes and Fields) was published in 1916.

VORDAGUR

Eftir Kristin Stefánsson

Hér er hönd mín, Vor!
Hugur léttir spor,
svo sem barn í sólskininu þínu.
Opna öll þín hlið
inn á lífs þíns svið
lát hið unga enn þá búa að sínu.

Láttu ljóðheim þinn
lykja um anda minn,
ber mér aftur bikar þinna veiga.
Láttu ljósblik þitt
lífið yngja mitt —
bittu því í skúr úr skini sveiga

SJÓDROPI

(Kveðið þegar höf. var fært glas fullt af sjó.)

Eftir Kristin Stefánsson

Nú skoða eg hér, ægi-breiða haf,
einn agnar-part af þér, svo voluglegu,
hinn salta dropa djúpi þínu af,
sem draup mér hingað frá þér óravegu.

Og þessi dropi er dropi úr æðum þér,
sem dundi og svall í þínum ólgulindum,
er hann við strönd í brimi bylti sér.
og brauzt þar fram í þínum ógna-myndum.

A DAY IN SPRING

Translated by Jakobina Johnson

Springtime, here's my hand!
Quickened thoughts expand,
Fleet as children in thy sunlight straying.
Life at rising tide
Seeks thy portals wide.
— Grant to youth its heritage of maying.

Realms of song untold
To my soul unfold.
Serve once more thy wine of glowing hours.
Let thy teeming light
Put my years to flight.
— Crown my life with sunshine through thy showers.

A DROP OF BRINE

(Bottled and brought by a friend from the Pacific Ocean.)

Translated by Jakobina Johnson

By man imprisoned, ocean wondrous vast,
An atom of thee reached me through the distance.
— A briny drop thy billows once held fast,
But yielded to my friend without resistance.

This drop has rested in thy mighty veins,
In sound and swell thy impulse wild receiving,
As in the surf it sang thy proud refrains,
Or, rose in giant forms thy bosom cleaving.

Hann lá í þinni þróttarstóru taug,
í þínum barka og afarsterku lungum,
og hjá þér hann þitt bylgju-brjóstið saug
og bar þitt nafn á allra storma tungum.

Og af því ég er alltaf fjarri þér,
en á þó drauma bernsku sálar minnar,
með glöðum huga hans til sný ég mér,
því hann er partur veldisdýrðar þinnar.

Thy very marrow was its dwelling place,
Thy lungs and monster throat their power sharing.
Thy billows nursed and fitted for the race:
Thy name among the winds of heaven bearing.

My footprints ever far from thee remained;
— But as my youthful dreams are not refuted,
I hail this drop with joyousness unfeigned —
— It shared thy sovereign glory undisputed.

KRISTJÁN N. JÚLÍUS
(b. 1860)

Kristján N. Júlíus ("K.N") was born at Akureyri in the North of Iceland. Eighteen years of age he emigrated to America. For several years he lived in Winnipeg, then for some time in Duluth, but for many years he has made his home in the Icelandic settlement at Mountain, North Dakota, where he has worked as a farm hand. He received only elementary education in Iceland, and is therefore largely self-taught. A volume of his poems and epigrams, Kviðlingar (Ditties), was published in 1920.

ÆFINTÝRI Á GÖNGUFÖR

Eftir Kristján N. Júlíus

Úr fimmtíu „centa" glasinu ég fengið gat ei nóg,
svo fleygði eg því á brautina og þagði; —
en tók upp aðra pyttlu og tappa úr henni dró
og tæmdi hana líka á augabragði.

Mér sortnaði fyrir augum og sýndist komin nótt
í sál og líkam virtist þrotinn kraftur.
Ég steyptist beint á hausinn og stóð upp aftur skjótt
og steyptist síðan beint á hausinn aftur.

Svo lá ég eins og skata, unz líða tók á dag, —
leit út sem mig enginn vildi finna. —
Ég hélt ég væri dauður og hefði fengið slag
og hefði kannske átt að drekka minna.

Þó komst ég samt á fætur og kominn er nú hér,
en kölski gamli missti vænsta sauðinn.
Og loksins hefur sannast á Lasarusi' og mér,
að lífið það er sterkara en dauðinn.

FEÐRATUNGAN

Eftir Kristján N. Júlíus

Þótt feðratungan flytji
oss fugla' og gígjuklið,
og brothljóð blárra kletta,
og brims og fossa nið,

TALE OF THE WAYSIDE

Translated by Guðmund J. Gislason

That half a dollar bottle held not enough for me;
Its empty form I viewed with consternation;
Another flask I opened and when its cork was free
I drank its contents without hesitation.

My eyes grew dim and strangely the day was
                                changed to night,
In body I felt weak, in spirit humble.
I toppled over headlong, but with my waning might
I quickly rose — then took another tumble.

I lay there still for hours for heavy was my yoke;
It did not seem my friends had missed me — really!
I thought that I was dead from an apoplectic stroke
And possibly had drunk a little freely.

At last my feet grew stronger, my eyes began to see,
And Satan lost a sheep he would'st devour;
And thus it has been proven on Lasarus and me,
That life surpasseth death in strength and power.

OUR NATIVE TONGUE

Translated by Skuli Johnson

Though our fore-fathers' language us dowers
With lyre-tones, singing-birds' calls,
And the sounds that abide in fell-bowers,'
And rhythms of seas and of falls,

er enskan eitthvað mýkri
með unaðshlýrri blæ, —
því íslenzkt mál á ekki
neitt orð, sem merkir „pie"

VIÐ GRÖF . . . .
Eftir Kristján N. Júlíus

Eg held, þú mundir hlæja dátt með mér
að horfa' á það, sem fyrir augun ber.
Þú hafðir ekki vanizt við það hér,
að vinir bæru þig á höndum sér.

En dauðinn hefur högum þínum breytt
og hugi margra vina til þín leitt;
í trú og auðmýkt allir hneigja sig,
og enginn talar nema vel um þig.

Still I deem that their English is sweeter,
More pleasing and charming — note why:
In the range of our tongue did you meet e'er
A word that could signify "p i e"?

AT THE FUNERAL OF . . . .

Translated by Bogi Bjarnason

I feel content that you would grin with me
Could you but witness what I hear and see.
For you were not accustomed — not your fate —
To be thus borne along by friends, in state.

But death has changed your status, so that now
Your friends assemble in your honor, bow
Their heads in faith, in grief, humility,
And all unite in speaking well of thee!

SIGURÐUR JÚLIUS JÓHANNESSON
(b. 1868)

Sigurður Júlíus Jóhannesson was born at Lækur in the South of Iceland. He was graduated from the College of Iceland in 1897. For some time he studied medicine at the Medical School in Reykjavík. In 1899 he emigrated to America. He continued his medical studies at the National Medical University in Chicago where he was given an M. D. degree in 1907. Since then he has been a practising physician, and now lives in Winnipeg. He has also engaged in journalism and has written a number of essays and articles. He published his first book, Sögur og kvæði (Stories and Poems), 1900—1903; a collected edition, Kvistir (Twigs), appeared in 1910.

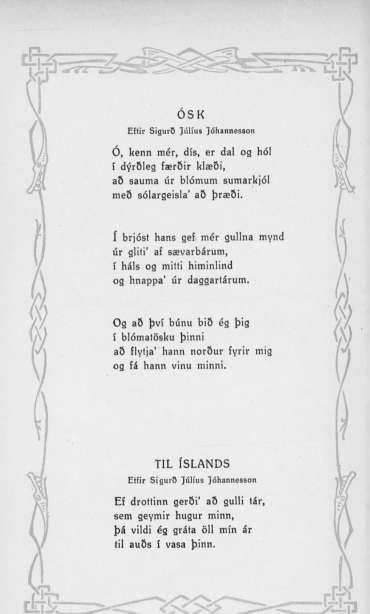

ÓSK

Eftir Sigurð Júlíus Jóhannesson

Ó, kenn mér, dís, er dal og hól
í dýrðleg færðir klæði,
að sauma úr blómum sumarkjól
með sólargeisla' að þræði.

Í brjóst hans gef mér gullna mynd
úr gliti' af sævarbárum,
í háls og mitti himinlind
og hnappa' úr daggartárum.

Og að því búnu bið ég þig
í blómatösku þinni
að flytja' hann norður fyrir mig
og fá hann vinu minni.

TIL ÍSLANDS

Etfir Sigurð Júlíus Jóhannesson

Ef drottinn gerði' að gulli tár,
sem geymir hugur minn,
þá vildi ég gráta öll mín ár
til auðs í vasa þinn.

A WISH

Translated by Skuli Johnson

Dear lass whose influence dale and height
With glorious raiment dowers,
Teach me to sew with threads of light
A summer dress of flowers.

Shape, for its breast, with subtle hands
The sheen of sea-waves shining,
Buttons of dew, and azure bands
for neck's and waist's entwining.

And when it's done the dress convey
Within your bag bloom-laden,
As north you go your gladsome way,
And give it to my maiden.

TO ICELAND

Translated by Christopher Johnston

If God would turn to gold the tears
With which my mind is blessed:
Then would I weep through all my years
To fill thy treasure-chest.

SÖNGUR SORGARINNAR

Eftir Sigurð Júlíus Jóhannesson

Í þínu nafni, guð, ég geng
og gegni skipan þinni;
þú veizt, að hvers manns hjartastreng
ég hefi' í gígju minni.

Og þegar dýpstu lífsins lög
ég leik að boði þínu,
mér finnst sem heimsins hjartaslög
ég heyri í brjósti mínu.

Og ef þín leyndu lög ég skil,
þú lézt mig starf þitt vinna,
og himnaríki er hvergi til
án hörpuslaga minna.

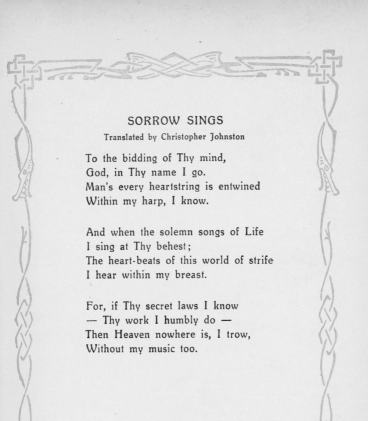

SORROW SINGS

Translated by Christopher Johnston

To the bidding of Thy mind,
God, in Thy name I go.
Man's every heartstring is entwined
Within my harp, I know.

And when the solemn songs of Life
I sing at Thy behest;
The heart-beats of this world of strife
I hear within my breast.

For, if Thy secret laws I know
— Thy work I humbly do —
Then Heaven nowhere is, I trow,
Without my music too.

GUTTORMUR J. GUTTORMSSON
(b. 1878)

Guttormur Jónsson Guttormsson was born at Icelandic River, Manitoba, Canada. His parents had emigrated to America from the eastern part of Iceland. Guttormsson only received public school education. He has for years been a farmer at Icelandic River. He is the only native of America who has published a book of poems in Icelandic. Two volumes of his have already appeared: Jón Austfirðingur (John from the Eastfirths), 1909, and Bóndadóttir (The Farmer's Daughter), 1920.

KANADA

Eftir Guttorm J. Guttormsson

Sem gjafvaxta mær, engum manni kær,
hún mændi fram á leið
með villimanns skart og metfé margt
hún mannsins hvíta beið,
með augunum blá um síðir sá
að siglandi kom hans skip,
og það var sem glans upp af höfði hans
og hátignarblær á hans svip.

Og hæversk og stillt hún var, en villt,
í vináttu föst og heil.
Að var hennar ást svo einlæg sást,
en aldrei hálf né veil,
hún faðmaði hann, sinn hvíta mann,
fann hjörtun saman slá;
hún opnaði barm og hug og hvarm
og himin allan sá.

Hann batt henni krans úr kornstanga fans,
en kórónu' úr lárvið sér,
því kóngsson var hann, sem þá kóngsdóttur fann
— þar kóngsríki síðan er.
Þau framleiða auð og blóm og brauð
og brúa dauðans hyl,
og þeirra höll er um víðan völl
með vorhimins ljós og yl.

Þau ala upp börn sín áframgjörn
með einkunn tigins manns,
en þeirra tryggð er á bjargi byggð
við bræður og móður hans;

CANADA

Translated by Jakobina Johnson

Expectant but free and lovely to see,
Her eyes on the future bent,
She waited his hand with treasures grand,
Adorned for the proud event.
When her dream came true, in the distant view
The white man's ship was seen,
Her exultant sight had him crowned with light
A hero of stately mien.

Refined was her face with courtly grace,
Though her manner was all untaught.
Her friendship was whole and pure her soul
And loyal her inmost thought.
She welcomed his charms with open arms,
And felt that their hearts were one.
Her vision had grown and all her own
A glorious day begun.

He wrought from the grains of her golden plains
A crown for his lady fair.
With the laurel crown of a just renown
He founded a kingdom there.
And the mountain walls of the royal halls
Were mirrored in lake and stream,
With their rooftree high as the azure sky
Where standards of freedom gleam.

Their sons prove the worth of their noble birth
As heroes in word and deed.
That reverence is due to their fathers too,
With them is a sacred creed.

Sé vopni beitt, þau öll eru eitt,
þau erfðu hetjumóð
úr föðurætt, sem aldrei rætt
skal upp, þó fjari blóð.

Og kær er hún oss sem kærast hnoss
hún Kanada móðir vor,
og lífsins dyr verða luktar fyr
en liggi á braut vor spor.
Í sókn og vörn það sýnum við börn,
að séum af stofni grein!
Þó greini oss mál, oss sameinar sál,
sem sönn er jafnan og ein.

GÓÐA NÓTT

Eftir Guttorm J. Guttormsson

Dúnalogn er allra átta,
allir vindar geims sig nátta,
nú er álfa heims að hátta,
hinztu geislar slokkna skjótt,
húmsins svarta silkiskýla
sveipar þekjur vorra býla,
upp er jörðin eins og hvíla
öllu búin. — Góða nótt!
Upp til hvíldar öllu búin
er nú jörðin. Góða nótt!

And a foeman's gun finds them all as one,
— They thrill to an ancient strain
Of a battle cry from the days gone by,
Whose glory shall never wane.

Devoted and true to their country new
Are Canada's sons today.
And death alone shall have claimed his own,
Ere they shall turn away.
With our strength untold which is tried and old,
Our country shall reach her goal,
Through the clearing haze and tongue and race
United in heart and soul.

GOOD NIGHT

Trnnslated by Jakobina Johnson

Stillness reigns. — The winds are sleeping.
All our world is bent on keeping
Tryst with night, whose wings are sweeping
From the west each ray of light.
Dusk, — a soft and silken cover
Over all is seen to hover
In its readiness to cover
All the drowsy world. — Good night.
Earth, — a restful bed inviting
All her tired to sleep. — Good night.

Langþrekuðum lýð er kærast
lágt að hvíla, endurnærast,
blunda lengi vel, sem værast
vekja taugum sínum þrótt,
yfir lofts og lagar strauma
líta Eden sinna drauma,
sólarbrautir svífa nauma
sælustundu. — Góða nótt!
Svífa stutta stundu brautir
stjarna og sólar. Góða nótt!

Tak þú, svefn, í ástararma
alla menn, sem þjást og harma,
legg þinn væng á lukta hvarma,
láttu öllum verða rótt,
leyf þeim, draumur, lengi að njóta
lífsins, sem í vöku brjóta
skipin sín í flök og fljóta
fram hjá öllu. — Góða nótt!
Þeim, sem fram hjá fegurð lífsins
fara í vöku. Góða nótt!

Streym þú, himins stilling, niður,
stattu við, þú, næturfriður.
Hugur fellur fram og biður,
funheitt andvarp lyftist hljótt:
Hætti allra sár að svíða,
sólar verði gott að bíða,
þurfi enginn kulda að kvíða,
komi sólskin. — Góða nótt!
Enginn þurfi' að óttast, komi
engill dagsins. Góða nótt!

Those who laboured long, untiring,
Hail this time of rest, — desiring
Strength renewed through sweet retiring,
— Welcome thoughts of short respite.
And through spaces real or seeming
Find the Eden of their dreaming,
Soar to starry ways, — redeeming
Hours of toil and pain. — Good night.
With the golden suns of heaven
As companion-stars. — Good night.

God of Sleep, descend embracing
All the weary souls, effacing
Pain and grief, — Thy pinions tracing
Airy ways in dreamy flight.
God of Dreams, prolong endearing
Scenes for all whose luckless steering
Wrecks their ships; — who go careering
Past all loveliness. — Good night.
Those who, drifting, miss the beauty
Of their waking hours. — Good night.

Peace of heav'n on all descending,
With this stillness softly blending
Here abide. — Our thoughts ascending
In a fervent prayer unite:
From the pain of wounds relieve us,
From the dread of cold reprieve us.
— May the joyous sun receive us
When the morning breaks. — Good night.
— All in peace await the radiant
Angel of the dawn. — Good night.

SÁL HÚSSINS

Eftir Guttorm J. Guttormsson

Sál hússins er eldur á arni
og eldur á lampakveik.
Ef farið er rangt með þann fjársjóð,
þá fyllist húsið af reyk,
og gluggarnir sortna af sóti
og syrtir að um rúm;
Þó úti álfröðull skíni,
er inni nótt og húm.

Ef út frá þeim arni og lampa
fer afvega hússins sál
og verður ei heft né hamin,
þá hleypur allt í bál;
að sál það allt hefur orðið,
sem æðir gönuskeið;
í blindni hún brennir til ösku
sinn bústað og deyr um leið.

Sál hússins er eldur á arni
og eldur á lampakveik.
Hún hnígur með sínu húsi
og hverfur loks í reyk.
Hvort er hennar ódauðleiki
þá aðeins fólginn í því,
Að allt af logar eldur,
deyr út og kviknar á ný?

THE SOUL OF THE HOUSE

Translated by Skuli Johnson

The Soul of the House is a Hearth's Lowe
And Light on a Lamp-wick that glows;
If men but mismanage this treasure
The Mansion all murky soon shows;
The Windows grow grimy and sooty
And Shadows descend on each Room;
Outside though the Sun-disk may shine well,
Within is sheer night and its gloom.

If, soaring from Hearth and from Home-lamp,
The Soul of the House leave her place,
And men can not hold her or hinder,
All quickly ascends in a blaze;
To soul has been altered whatever
Its path in abandon on plies;
In blindness she burns down to ashes
Her Home, and then likewise she dies.

The Soul of the House is a Hearth's Lowe
And Light on a Lamp-wick that glows;
She sinks down to death with her home, and
In smoke disappears at the close.
Is this then her essence eternal
Unfolded for all men to view:
Forever a Fire upflashes,
Dies out, and arises anew?

EINAR PÁLL JÓNSSON
(b. 1881)

Einar Páll Jónsson was born at Háreksstaðir in the East of Iceland. He is largely self-educated. For years he has lived in Winnipeg, occupying himself with journalistic work. At present he is the editor of the weekly L ö g b e r g . He has written a number of essays and articles as well as lyric poetry. A volume of his poems, Θ r æ f a l j ó ð (Songs of the Deserts), appeared in 1915.

ÞJÓNN LJÓSSINS

Eftir Einar P. Jónsson

Hamrarnir skelfa' ekki hug þess manns,
er helgaður þjónustu sannleikans
leitar til ljóssins hæða
að lind hinna dýpstu fræða.

Útverðir dagroðans eggja hann,
þann andlega brattsækna konung-mann
að margklifa björgin bláu — —
af brúninni skyggnast háu.

Þar mótast hans andi er morguninn
mynnist við austurhimininn,
er ljósfljótin líða að sævi
með ljóðklið í heiðisblævi.

Að lýsa' inn í myrkrin er löngun hans,
og ljóma upp skammdegi syrgjandans. —
Hann langar að lækna sárin
með ljósi og þerra tárin.

Um aldirnar stendur þar óðal hans,
þess einbeitta talsmanns sannleikans —
í álfunni óðs og hljóma,
við eilífan dýrðarljóma.

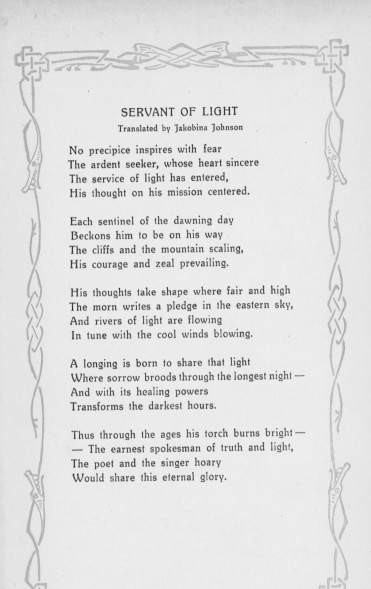

SERVANT OF LIGHT

Translated by Jakobina Johnson

No precipice inspires with fear
The ardent seeker, whose heart sincere
The service of light has entered,
His thought on his mission centered.

Each sentinel of the dawning day
Beckons him to be on his way
The cliffs and the mountain scaling,
His courage and zeal prevailing.

His thoughts take shape where fair and high
The morn writes a pledge in the eastern sky,
And rivers of light are flowing
In tune with the cool winds blowing.

A longing is born to share that light
Where sorrow broods through the longest night —
And with its healing powers
Transforms the darkest hours.

Thus through the ages his torch burns bright —
— The earnest spokesman of truth and light,
The poet and the singer hoary
Would share this eternal glory.

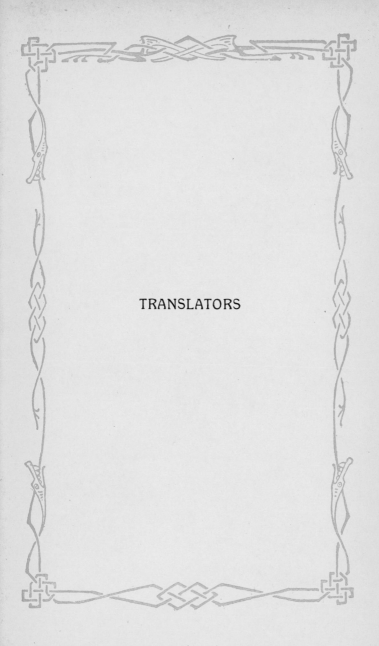

TRANSLATORS

MAGNÚS A. ARNASON

was born and brought up in Iceland, but has for a number of years lived in America. His home is in Point Roberts, Washington. He is a sculptor, but is also deeply interested in literature. Original poems of his in the Icelandic have appeared in the weekly Heimskringla. He has published two volumes of Icelandic translations from Togore's Poetry.

BOGI BJARNASON

was born near Mountain, North Dakota, of Icelandic parentage. He lives in St. Vital, Manitoba. He is largely a self-educated man. He has principally interested himself in journalism, and has been the publisher and editor of various papers in Saskatchewan. He frequently contributes to the Icelandic weekly Heimskringla. He is an able writer of short stories.

PAUL BJARNASON,

brother of Bogi Bjarnason, was also born near Mountain, North Dakota. He lives in Wynyard, Saskatchewan. He studied at the University of North Dakota. He has interested himself in journalism and literature. His English translations from Icelandic poetry, as well as his original poems in the Icelandic have appeared in the Icelandic weeklies in Winnipeg.

SIR WILLIAM A. CRAIGIE,

one of the editors-in-chief of the great Oxford English Dictionary, is well known to English-speaking readers. He was born and brought up in Scotland. He studied at St. Andrews University and at Oxford University. He also spent a year in Copenhagen studying Scandinavian languages, especially Icelandic. For a number of years he was professor at Oxford: now he is at the University of Chicago, editing the Historical Dictionary of American English. Sir William has written a number of articles and several books on Scandinavian subjects. We mention only his excellent monograph The Icelandic Sagas. He collaborated with Sir Edmund Gosse in editing The Oxford Book of Scandinavian Verse.

RUNÓLFUR FJELDSTED

(1879—1921) was born in Iceland, but came to America as a child. He studied at Wesley College, Winnipeg, the Lutheran

Theological Seminary in Chicago, Harvard University, and at the University of Chicago.

For some time he taught in the department of classics at Carthage College, Illinois. He translated into English a number of poems from the Icelandic; these appeared in both Canadian and American publications. He also wrote poetry in English.

ERL. G. GILLIES

was born and brought up in Iceland, but came to America when about twenty years of age. He is a sheet-metal worker by trade, and lives in New Westminster, British Columbia. He is very largely self-educated, but a man of wide reading. Several of his translations from Icelandic poetry have appeared in the weekly Heimskringla.

GUDMUND J. GISLASON

was born in Iceland, but came to America at the age of five. He studied at the University of Manitoba, the University of North Dakota, and at Illinois Medical College. He also studied medicine in London and Vienna. For a number of years he has been a practising physician and surgeon in Grand Forks, North Dakota. He is well versed in Icelandic literature. His translations from Icelandic poetry, and his poems in English have appeared in various American publications.

JAKOBINA JOHNSON

came with her parents from Iceland to Canada at the age of six. She was educated in the public schools of Manitoba. She lives in Seattle, Washington. Her numerous translations from Icelandic poetry have appeared in the Icelandic weeklies in Canada and in many American magazines. She is also a poet in her own right, and a large number of her poems in the Icelandic have been printed in Canadian-Icelandic papers and periodicals.

SKULI JOHNSON

was brought by his parents from Iceland to Canada when one year old. He studied at the University of Manitoba and at Oxford University, as Rhodes Scholar. For a number of years he was professor of classics at Wesley College, Winnipeg, and Dean of the Faculty of Arts. He is now professor of classics at the University of Manitoba. A number of his trans-

lations from Icelandic poetry have appeared in the Icelandic-
American weeklies and in American publications.

CHRISTOPHER JOHNSTON
(d. 1927) came to America when a child. He translated several
Icelandic poems into English; these appeared in the Canadian-
Icelandic weeklies. He also wrote a number of poems in English; these were published in Canadian and American papers.

EIRÍKR MAGNÚSSON
(1833—1913) was born and brought up in Iceland. He studied
at the College of Iceland and graduated from the Theological
School in Reykjavík. He was a librarian at Cambridge University and Fellow of Trinity College. In collaboration with
William Morris he translated many of the Icelandic sagas into
English. He wrote numerous articles on Scandinavian mytho-
logy and Northern lore. He translated Pilgrim's Progress
and The Tempest into Icelandic.

VILHJALMUR STEFANSSON,
the renowned explorer, was born at Arnes, Manitoba, of Icelandic parentage. He studied at the University of North Dakota,
the University of Iowa, and Harvard University. His extensive arctic explorations have brought him much fame and
numerous honors. He is a very productive writer — the author
of several books and a great number of articles in various
periodicals. He is a lecturer of note. His translations from
Icelandic poetry were embodied in two articles on Icelandic
literature, published in Poet-Lore in 1904.

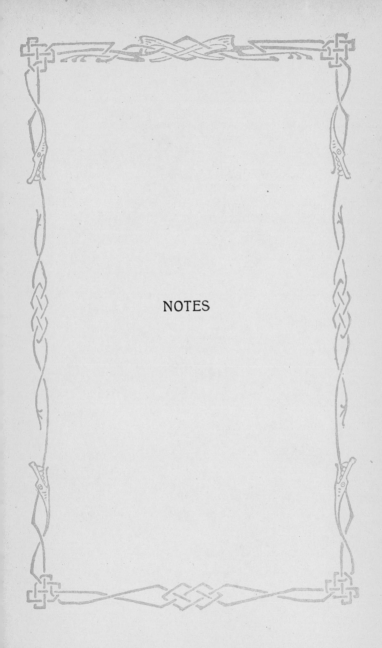

NOTES

ICELAND. Steeds of the tide, a kenning (poetic circum-
locution) meaning ships.

TO THE "RIVER'S SLOPE". The River's Slope (Fljóts-
hlíð or Fleetlithe), in southern Iceland, is noted for its
scenic beauty as well as for its many historic places. These
include Hlíðarendi, the home of Gunnar in Njáls saga.
Bjarni Thórarersen was brought up at this famous home-
stead.

ICELAND (Jónas Hallgrímsson). Frón originally means land;
in modern poetry, especially in patriotic songs, it is a
pet name for Iceland. Icelandic students in Copenhagen,
1763, were the first to use the word in this sense. Cf. R.
Cleasby and G. Vigfússon: An Icelandic-English
Dictionary.

The Althing, the Icelandic Parliament, was held at Þingvellir (Thing-plains) in south-western Iceland from 930
until 1800. Almanna gorge (Almanna-gjá) forms the entrance to the Thing-plains. Oxar river (Öxará) flows partly
through the Almanna gorge and then on across the plains.
The scenery at Þingvellir is renowned for its grandeur.
See W. G. Collingwood and J. Stefánsson: A Pilgrimage
to the Saga-Steads of Iceland, Ulverston, W.
Holmes, 1899.

Þorgeir was the Law-Speaker (lögsögumaður) when
Christianity was introduced in Iceland in the year 1000.
Gunnar is Gunnar of Hlíðarendi (See the poem "Gunnar's
Holm"). Hedinn is Skarp-hedinn (See the poem "Skarp-
hedinn Among the Flames"). Gissur and Geir play an
important part in Njáls saga.

Snorri's booth (Snorrabúð). A reference to Snorri goði
Þorgrímsson (d. 1031) and not to the historian, poet, and
statesman Snorri Sturluson (d. 1241).

Lögberg the sacred. From Lögberg (The Mount of
Laws) the Law-speaker proclaimed the laws and decisions.
It was the centre of the Althing.

GUNNAR'S HOLM. The poem is based on an incident in Njáls saga. (Cf. chapter 74 in G. W. Dasent's translation). The scene is laid in southern Iceland. Shortly before writing the poem, Hallgrímsson had journeyed through these historic regions, which once upon a time were fertile, but had now been laid waste through floods. Only a small patch of land, grown with grass, remained. Tradition held this to be the place where Gunnar returned home. (Cf. introductory note to poem, Fjölnir, 1838, pp. 31—32).

Frosti and Fjalar are two dwarfs.

The halberd is Gunnar's favorite weapon, his famed atgeir — a spear and axe combined.

Coalbeard is Kolskeggr, Gunnar's brother.

ON SWINES' DALE. Kjartan is Kjartan Ólafsson, the hero of the tragic Laxdæla saga. See translation by Muriel A. C. Press, in the Temple Classics, or The Story of the Laxdalers, by R. Proctor.

'NEATH "DARKSOME FELLS". Darksome Fells (Svörtuloft) are dark and gloomy rock cavities on the extreme end of Snæfellsnes in western Iceland.
Beloved scion of our island-race. A reference to Jón Jónsson, a teacher in the Latin school at Bessastaðir. He was drowned off Svörtuloft in March 1817 .

KING SVERRIR. This is King Sverrir Sigurðsson who ruled Norway from 1177 to 1202. He is especially noted for his stern opposition to the Pope and the clergy. See Knut Gjerset: History of the Norwegian People, Vol. I, pp. 376—405. Also The Saga of King Sverrir of Norway, translatet by J. Sephton, London, 1899.
Wakeful. "Wakeful" (andvaka) was Sverrir's famous battle-trumpet.

EGGERT ÓLAFSSON. Eggert Ólafsson (1726—1768) was an Icelandic naturalist, philologist, poet, and patriot. With his bride he was drowned in Breiðafjörður on May 30, 1768.

They were on their way to the farm of Hofstaðir on the south side of Snæfellsnes. See Islandica, Vol. XVI, 1925. Scaur (Skor) is "a landing place on the north shore of Breiðafjörður, going directly south towards Snæfellsnes" (Islandica, Vol. XVI, p. 18).

THE CATARACT. The Cataract (Dettifoss), in nothern Iceland, is the country's largest waterfall, and one of the largest in Europe.

SKARPHEDINN AMONG THE FLAMES. The subject-matter of the poem is from Njáls saga. (Cf. chapters 128 and 129 in Dasent's translation, particularly the latter). Berg-thora is Njal's wife, Kari their son-in-law, Helgi and Grimur their sons.

Battle-Ogre (Rimmu-gýgr) was Skarphedinn's battle-axe, his favorite weapon.

NEARING COLD DALE. Cold Dale (Kaldadalur) is a mountain trail through a pass between Langjökull and Ok in the interior of Iceland, used on journeys from the South to the North.

THORVALDUR THORODDSEN. Thorvaldur Thoroddsen (1855—1921) was an Icelandic geologist and geographer. He made extensive research journeys through Iceland, studying geological conditions and the physical geography of the country. He wrote a number of authoritative works on these subjects.

YOU WOMEN. "Lilja" by Eysteinn. A famous Icelandic religious poem by the monk Eysteinn Ásgrimsson (d. 1361). See Lilja (The Lily), edited, with metrical translation, notes, and glossary, by Eiríkr Magnússon, London, 1870.